THE OFFICIAL
SLOANE RANGER
Diary

THE · FIRST · GUIDE · TO · THE · SLOANE · YEAR

ANN BARR & PETER YORK

TO THE UNKNOWN SLOANE

There are no famous Sloanes
(unless fame was thrust upon them by
marriage, inheritance or a monumental blunder).
Sloanes do not know how to lay down a task,
so every new thing (Sony Walkman, elephant polo, ceroc)
just adds to their duties.
They are far too busy
keeping up to the mark
to ever make a mark.
But why be an individual when you can serve life?
The following pages explain how Sloanes tackle the Task.

EBURY PRESS
LONDON

Published by Ebury Press
National Magazine House
72 Broadwick Street
London W1V 2BP

First impression 1983

© The National Magazine Company Limited
and (text only) Peter York and Ann Barr 1983

ISBN 0 85223 296 9 (paper)
ISBN 0 85223 355 8 (cased)

Editor: Susie Ward

Design: Harry Green

Artists: Merrily Harpur
         Natacha Ledwidge

The authors would like to state that
the information contained in this book
was checked as rigorously as possible
before going to press. Neither the authors
nor the publishers can take responsibility
for any changes which may have
occurred since, nor for any other variance
of fact from that recorded here
in good faith.

Filmset in Great Britain by
MFK Typesetting Ltd
Printed and bound in Great Britain by
The University Press, Cambridge

Contributors

Many writers provided words, observations, jokes and facts for this book. *The Official Sloane Ranger Diary* owes an enormous amount to:

SUE CARPENTER

and also to:

Jane Abdy, Amanda Atha, Antony Atha, Simon Arscott, Diana Avebury, Iris Banham-Lee, Mollie Baines, Greig Barr, Mary Bass, Robin Brackenbury, Robin Bryer, Susan Campbell, Jean Carpenter, Michael Carpenter, Mirabel Cecil, Nicholas Coleridge, Danny Danziger, William Davies, Elma Dayrell, Tim de Lisle, Paolo Filo della Torre, Annie Dent, Neville Dent, Sarah Drummond, Charlotte Du Cann, Ian Dunlop, Andrew Edmunds, Bryony Edmunds, Henry Elwell, Jenny Fabian, Sophy Fisher, David Galloway, Anthony Gardner, Maurice Graham, Priscilla Greville, Mardi Harrison, Susannah Hawarden, Hugh Johnson, John Julian, Roddy Martine, Victoria Mather, Mary Muir, Deirdre Mulloy, Patrea More Nisbett, Patrick O'Connor, Mary Oliver, Andrew Pfeiffer, Godfrey Pilkington, Nick Rosen, Teresa Sackville-West, Alistair Scott, Julian Seaman, Richard Sharpe, Caroline Silver, Clare Stourton, Michael Stourton, Douglas Sutherland, Simon Taylor, Katie Tute, Arthur Ward, Susie Ward, Sophy Webster, Claire Wickham, Michael Williams, Jenny Wilson, Michael Yardley.

The words are greatly cheered up, the authors feel, by the design of HARRY GREEN.

CONTENTS

Page 10   JANUARY

January brings the Blizzard –
Not the snow, *the teenage ball* –
And though the weather isn't wizard
One must *shoot* though glass do fall
And bag *cock pheasants*,
Sale Christmas presents,
One's unbroken presence
At racecourses, socs and clubs.
The chilliest chill's financial
But being a member is essential
So one pays those giant *subs*.

Page 22   FEBRUARY

February brings the snow.
Nothing's new but *point-to-pointing*.
One is feeling pretty low.
Everything is disappointing:
Ice bans hunting,
Lent kills drinking,
Exercises start tums shrinking,
Cruft's don't recognise one's *dog*.
Time for the winter holiday:
'In February one's away.'
Only *stallions* enjoy their job.

Page 32   MARCH

In March one's bulbs can feel a stir
And car-boot *picnics* bloom again.
At *Cheltenham* and Doncaster
We study *form*, though all in vain.
Eights are *rowing*,
Caroline *sowing*,
Hunting ends when the corn starts
   growing,
Après-skiers hit the piste.
It's time to get out clothes for *cricket*
And to book the summer *tickets*
As hostesses prepare their list.

Page 40   APRIL

In April life is not just *Flat*:
The National's a must for us.
Henry in his *fishing* hat
Casts his bread on waters illustrious.
It's the *Easter hols*,
Badminton trials,
Cleaning the jewels,
Weekly visits to *the dressmaker*.
We drink pink *Kir* from a glass darkly
As *debs* start their *Season* at the Berkeley.
(Mums fear rivals will overtake her.)

Page 54   MAY

In May we sip a bottomless *Pimm's*
On lawns, in *punts*, at *Oxford and
   Cambridge*.
The *English asparagus season* begins.
The Portrait Painters know what our name
   is.
To the *opera* we go,
Smiths Lawn for *polo*,
The *Chelsea Flower Show*.
We feel quite weak with anticipation.
It's not love or *tennis* –
The real thrill's when it's
Time for the marquee erection.

Page 66   JUNE

In June the promise is fulfilled.
Summer honours a cheque signed
   Sloane.
Eton's in flower, the champers chilled,
Caterers lift salmon off the bone.
The Derby is run for us,
Ascot is sumptuous,
The *wedding* was fun for us.
Oxbridge colleges have a *ball*.
'New bollocks please,' says *Wimbledon*.
Hostesses say 'They will be done.'
Henley's the poshest picnic of all.

Page 80   JULY

In July boarders come home to roost –
Except the ones who are in *drug clinics*
(Sloanes love to mix with the upper crust
But some are crumbs with horrible
   gimmicks).
It's the *Queen's garden parties*,
Congregating with smarties,
The start of the raspb'ries.
The season is petering out in Mayfair.
Sloanes go down to *Goodwood*.
To work now is no good.
It's one's duty to play at the Game Fair.

Page 86   AUGUST

August is the dispersal month.
All Sloanes know that *Cowes* have *balls*.
If one hasn't got a place in the sunth
One must be out on the *grouse* moors
On knickerbocker glorious twelfth
To preserve one's *spaniel's* health –
One does not do things for oneself.
One *stalks* in *Scotland's* wettest heather.
Henry's been left on his own,
So how can the Sloanes *conceive a son*???
Don't let's be serious in this weather.

Page 94   SEPTEMBER

September's coupled to the *school* train.
Parents seek *educational shrinks*.
They have a hard time finding the brain
Let alone what the young Sloane thinks.
The *City* gets a new Lord Mayor.
Cub-hunting seems hardly fair.
Time for a Bloody Mar-y.
It's cool enough for a reel ball
After a Highland gathering.
Two days on Skye's the limit.
The Scottish Season's in the village hall.

Page 102   OCTOBER

In October we work for *charity*,
Dancing, drinking – we give all night.
And they've harnessed *child sociability*
To get the toddler's mite.
The chairwoman's inveigling,
The beagles start *beagling*,
The *barristers* eagling,
And the *universities go up*.
At the political conference
Our side deserves compliments.
The others ought to be shot.

Page 112   NOVEMBER

Remember, remember, a Sloane is a
   member.
In November that means of a *shoot*.
If you aren't a *pheasant*-slaughterer
You're cleaning your *hunting* boots.
It's *Beaujolais nouveau*,
The Earl's Court *Ski Show*,
Rams having their go,
But Caroline's still *pruning* trees.
November is exceedingly hard
If you keep in touch by Christmas card
A hundred of them overseas.

Page 120   DECEMBER

December's when we all go home
(The worse for wear for *office parties*).
Peace at Christmas isn't Sloane –
Animals are where one's heart is.
Racing's over the sticks,
One *glühweins* till sick,
There's the *presents* to pick –
Years have walls, and we're up against it.
The boss looks like thunder.
There's no nursery fender.
But fun will begin again – Sloanes sense it.

A year in Sloaneland

A season a day keeps the doctor away

'Time – like – an ev – er – rolling stream! Bears – all – its – sons – a – way. They fly for – got – ten. As a dream – dies at the opening day.'

So you sing in church. But you don't believe it. To you, time is not rolling away like a digital watch; it is circling around like a watch with hands, and will return undiminished next year at the start of the new season.

The *season*! That is what Sloanes believe in. For other people, the year has been ironed out flat and given a 52-week guarantee of stolid mundaneness. But that has no place in the mind of the Sloane, where at least 30 seasons jostle thrillingly – each uncomfortable, unpredictable and possibly fatal ('Had a Frenchman next to him in the butt . . .').

Like all those with lazy minds, Sloanes love a deadline, and the seasons provide it. You get your horse/rod/foredeck gorilla/oyster knife ready for each glorious start. You're off . . . the pace is terrific . . . you and your rival are neck and neck . . . it's the last fence . . . YOU FEEL YOURSELF FALLING . . . the season is over.

But you don't mourn. Cricket is looming, and *The* Season with 'The dance we're sharing with two other mothers', and 'We *always* take Coronation Chicken to Glyndebourne', and the Royal Academy, and on and on, round and round, forever and ever.

Sloanes, seeing themselves as in touch with the *pulse of Nature* (although they would find such an expression D. H. Lawrence-ish), do not hold with anything *out of season*. The sole exception is avocados, acceptable all year round. Anything else that achieves over-six-month availability is patently suspect.

Sloane Rangers feel themselves to be on good terms with death – another of the things modern people are doing their best to eradicate. Sloanes are content to be part of the nitrogen cycle, seeing it all as what Americans call 'serial immortality', as living on through *your* people. Death, after all, is the *sine qua non* of decay which, in its lesser manifestations, can lend so much to game, wine, cheese, houses and furniture.

Many Sloane Rangers get killed – after all, you are the fast-driving, hard-riding, heavy-drinking set. But you have killed plenty of animals in your time.

Your sporting occasions are full of Sloanes in iden-tical clothes, but they are drawn up in two opposing camps: the Hooray Henrys And Other Amateurs versus the Keen. The Keen hate 'people who hunt (shoot/sail/come to point-to-points) for fun'. But as all Sloanes turn out for Sloane events, the Keen have to put up with the Unkeen littered all over the place – unless it's foul weather which, thank God, keeps them away.

The event-full calendar

To avoid the doldrums, Sloanes like to go abroad in January or February and in early August. But abroad is not as lively (in the *Sloane* meaning of the word) as Britain, so you have to be careful. There is nothing more frightful than a place that is 'out of season', except a place chock-a-block with hoi polloi.

Back in Britain again, as the Sloane population increases, so does the pressure on Sloane places like Badminton and the Isle of Wight ferry (you book in January for Cowes in August). The great thing is to keep the hoi polloi out. You foil them by Sloanedom's very elaborate, stuffy, long-term book-ing procedures. By the time Instant Society (just add money) thinks about Windlebum, in May, the ballot is long closed and the waiting list is solid Sloane.

The idea of planning, of planting seeds which ages later bear fruit, of laying things down, is central to Sloanedom. Your education, your financial arrange-ments, your wine, your passion for bloodlines, even your food (Caroline freezes and bottles like a maniac) are all examples of planned, *deferred* gratification.

It is as a reaction to the discipline and rigidity of their code that Sloanes drink to get drunk, throw chocolate mousse, love plastic-dog-mess jokes and try to behave worse than the Sloanes-next-door. They know they have to take the road west at eight sharp tomorrow, them and their senior hangover.

To Rangers, their diary is a servant of the Great God Planning. The Sloane's diary is the epicentre of his/her social whirlpool. It is a second, secret life written in invisible ink in the *Economist*'s red morocco number, with its selling periods and clutter of finan-cial markets. Caroline has *Harpers & Queen*'s black leather diary, but she deplores its devaluing church dates like Shrove Tuesday and Ash Wednesday, and leaving out the phases of the moon. The ancient festivals demand attention. It could be 1880 or 1920. The physical world, and with it the Sloane world, is still turning at the same pace.

	JAN	FEB	MAR	APR	MAY	JUNE	JULY	AUG	SEPT	OCT	NOV	DEC
Horse covering												
Sheep covering												
Human covering												
Cubbing												
Hunting												
Beagling												
Grouse shooting												
Pheasant shooting												
Fishing												
Flat racing												
National Hunt racing												
Three-day eventing												
Point-to-pointing												
Picnics												
Punting												
Rowing												
Polo												
Tennis												
Asparagus												
Strawberries/ Raspberries												
London deb season												
Scottish season												
Little season												
Wedding												
School												
Holidays		Skiing						Corfu				
Drinks	Glühwein	Chisky	Sloe gin	Kir	Pimm's	Champagne	Pimm's	Retsina	Ouzo	Bloody Mary	Beaujolais Nouveau	Glühwein

What's what and who's who

Henry

Caroline

Sophie

Jamie

Edward

Emma

Alasdair Wallace-Dunbar
(major Ret.)

Sloanes can feel grass beneath the pavement. Though modern farming methods have speeded maturing in some plants and animals, Sloanes *hate* the battery chicken principle. Their seasons are tied to wild plants, wild animals and birds. 'In it goes, out it comes,' as Farmer Henry says.

The Sloane cyclic concept (unlike that of Marx) always comes back to reproduction. Even Sloane humans breed in the right season, between August and mid-November: otherwise their progeny will be the wrong age for the Michaelmas term. (That is *something* to write down for the first fortnight in August.)

Thus 'the season' for any species is its peak of promise, the burst into adulthood when the grape or girl, racehorse or woodcock is just ripe, 'comes out', shows what it can do and is picked (or marries, wins or is shot). Your quarry may be a husband or a bowl of raspberries. It could be a silk shirt in the sales or a fish in the salmon season. It's exciting, fun, sexy and a million miles more

natural than watching *The Good Life* on television.

The Sloane family: who's who

The *Sloane* family moved from Fulham about four years ago and now live on the Wiltshire-Berkshire border.

Henry is 45, and getting on fairly well at Macroe Watson, a medium-sized commodity brokers. He commutes up to London. Shooting and fishing are his favourite pursuits – he can't understand Caroline's predilection for hunting.

Caroline is 42 and *amazing* at running the house, coping with Jamie, Sophie, Edward and Emma, and Polly (18hh) *and* helping with Riding for the Disabled *and* cooking for charity do's *and* transporting old ladies to weekly tea-parties *and* popping up to London . . . .

Jamie, 18 in April, is doing A-levels this summer at Eton. After Oxbridge (he's trying for Christ Church), he'll have a year off to bum around Australia.

Sophie, Jamie's twin, is at secretarial college in Oxford, and is Coming Out in May. Then she's going to do a quick Cordon Bleu and zoom off to Val as a chalet girl.

Edward is 13 in March. He takes his Common Entrance exams in June. Henry hopes he'll make it to Eton – otherwise it's Milton Abbey or Pangbourne. He calls himself Harold Azlett.

Emma is 12 in July. She takes her Common Entrance exams in February. She's trying for St Mary's Wantage, Tudor Hall or Cranborne. Pony Club mad.

Major Wallace-Dunbar is Caroline's father. A widower, ex-Gordon Highlanders, he runs the family estate near Beauly, Inverness-shire.

Elizabeth is Caroline's sister; *John* is her husband; *Harry*, *Annabel* and *Charlotte* are their children.

Simon is Annabel's fiancé.

Labby is Henry's labrador.

Hannah is Caroline's border terrier bitch.

Polly is Caroline's hunter.

Sloane going-out clothes, A to J

Show respect for the occasion

It doesn't matter what you wear in private – alone in your bedroom, you could even get away with the dreaded anorak, the sure sign of a hoi polloi. But for going out, there are *rules*. To dress like a noovo is bad, but to make no attempt at correct dress is worse. Jeans and a****k show 1) disrespect, 2) that you are putting no money into the sport. At least the noovos do that. To Sloanes, the question you refrain from snapping at cheeky grockles is not 'Do you realise who I am?' but 'Do you realise *where* you are?'

These ten correct kits will take you anywhere. You might be named Dowdiest Person, but at least you'll look like a lady or gentleman. (These rules hold for all except Edward, who is not an iconoclast, but just *hates* clothes. Anyway, he's usually hidden away at school.)

A for amateur. Who else would go in for chilly muddy masochism like watching point-to-points in February and going to pub meets?

Henry
Old British Warm or sheepskin, ancient fawn or mustard cords

green wellies or walking shoes

tweed cap from Herbie J

Hunters' Improvement Society tie (very recherché)

binoculars (or Field Glasses as Henry calls them)

Jamie
Barbour

Guernsey

trilby

jeans or cords

major public school scarf

wellies

binoculars

Caroline
Husky or sheepskin, silk scarf on head with man's trilby over it like a Peruvian peasant, small pheasant feather in the hatband (scarf hideous, double hideous with hat on top)

jeans or cords

Derriboots or Hunter wellies

binoculars

Sophie
One of Henry's horrid old jerseys

big woolly scarf

man's baggy overcoat

stripy trousers tucked into suede boots caked with mud

trilby ('We all wear trilbies except Daddy. Caps are for codgers and stupid old Edward')

B for Badminton, Burghley and so on. Tidier version of A (the Queen might see you)

Henry
Add tweed jacket and cavalry twill trousers, or tweed suit

madly polished old brown shoes

cap

madly polished old brown stick

binoculars

Jamie
Tiltier trilby

tweed jacket

cords

shirt and tie

V-neck lambswool pullover

Caroline
Husky

Hermès scarf

tweed skirt

pearls

Derriboots, Lady Northamptons or madly polished old brown walking shoes if over 50

shooting stick

binoculars

Sophie
As A but add pearl necklace and earrings, and substitute Jamie's Barbour

no trilby – airing the wild hair

C for church, Cheltenham, Chelsea Flower Show

Henry
Tweed or worsted suit in winter, grey suit in summer

trilby

covert coat (rhymes with lover; the T is silent, as in jig a lot)

Caroline
Tweed suit, velvet beret with brooch in winter

Navy skirt, velvet blazer in summer; skirt displays jutting Sloane bum

Jamie
Grey flannel suit (or whatever his school suit is)

Sophie
Loden coat

pearls

coloured tights

(when racing, borrows the family binoculars: 'Men seldom make passes at girls without 7×40 glasses')

What's what and who's who

D for a smart Do: cocktail party, City lunch

Henry
Striped blue or grey suit

coloured silk handkerchief in breast pocket (some Sloanes still swear by white – 'Coloured is charlie')

striped shirt

Jamie
His suit

striped shirt

striped or polka-dot tie

Caroline
Silk or wool printed dress (no one else wears printed dresses anymore, but Caroline can be seen in hers at Covent Garden, the Mansion House and other museums of dress)

pearls

matching draped hat, in the daytime, if over 65

Sophie
Pretty white blouse

full Monsoon silky skirt or floral skirt (or Laura Ashley-type dress)

coloured tights

court shoes

pearls

More vampy in the evening: jazzier jewellery, pointed stilettos

E is for evening dress no 2: Black tie

Henry
Prefers double-breasted dinner jacket, as s-b makes too much parade of shirt and cummerbund (not to mention expanding pot), both areas where noovos commit grave errors. D-b more discreet – looks like a suit

cotton piqué shirt, never nylon

matt silk tie – straight-ended, never butterfly

(MFH Henrys wear pink tailcoats at the Hunt Ball)

Jamie
Black dinner jacket from Distressed Gentlefolks jumble/ Oxfam/trendy Sloane second-hand shop like Biggles in Salisbury, full of landowner clothes. Not white, unless geniune old sharkskin

colourful patterned or flashing bow-tie as an alternative to black

Caroline
Long full dress, 4 row pearl choker

hair a sculptured monument to the ladies' hairdresser's dying art

Sophie
The Dress: Bright-coloured strapless calf-length taffeta

dangly diamanté earrings

Daddy's DJ on top

a shock of hair

F for full evening dress: White tie

Henry
Knows he looks like a gentleman: 'Show me your white-tie buttons and I will tell you who you are'

his tails are not too long (waiters), his trousers are not too wide (commissionaires), his cuff links and studs not too fancy (noovos). He's glad he inherited it all

Caroline
Low scoop-neck top, big taffeta skirt
        or
embossed print full-length dress that looks like the drawing-room curtains

glittering earrings like bits of the hall chandelier

4-row choker again

dowdy gold shoes and bag she has had 10 years

Jamie
He inherited it all too. Might substitute Bullingdon or similar jacket and tie

Cousin Nicholas (in Army)
Full mess kit (makes Sophie go weak at the knees)

Sophie
Full-length strapless taffeta dress

Butler & Wilson drop pearl earrings

patent court shoes

hair toned down

G for grass-sitting clothes in the summer,

to watch polo, tennis, cricket. Mustn't compete with the spectacle

Henry
Brooks Bros jacket or blazer

grey flannels

Caroline
Cotton jacket

Liberty shirt

pleated skirt

not sandals – Sloanes do not wear sandals in the daytime. The Sloane sandal is the espadrille

Jamie
Grey flannels

white shirt

school team jersey

Sophie
Bright, flouncy cotton skirt

T-shirt

Jamie's sleeveless cricket jersey

one or two studded belts ('I thought punk was dead' growls Henry)

H for Henry's panama worn here. Henley, Goodwood, Fourth of June. Now you *are* the spectacle

Henry
Cuts a dudicious jash in Pimm's weather in grey flannel suit or, for Henley white flannels. With the whites goes a gaudy school, college or club blazer for any sport you or your father achieved prominence in. (MCC makes conquest anywhere)

Caroline
Summer dress

light wool or velvet blazer

straw hat with flowers or even ostrich

Jamie
Grey flannels and blue-and-white striped seersucker blazer
or
suit for Fourth of June

White flannels, blue or rowing blazer and tie, boater or panama for Henley

Sophie
Laura Ashley billowing striped drop-waisted frock, flat pumps (heels get stuck in the grass)

optional straw hat or boater with streamers

J for June Ascot

Henry
As for weddings

Jamie and Charles
As for weddings

Caroline
Silk dress and coat or one of Lady Tryon's Kanga Collection (doesn't need dry cleaning)

gloves

pearls

best *unfussy* hat

Sophie
Long-sleeved silky dress with detail at neck and contrasting belt. (It's the kind of thing Diana wears to official functions – floaty, smart and far too grown-up. But Caroline will *not* be disgraced by her daughter at Royal Ascot. She ends up looking just like Caro. There's little to choose between them from behind – except the *size* of the behind)

I for I'm a gentleman in his daytime tails

Henry
Black morning suit for very grand funerals (black waistcoat), Epsom Owners' and Trainers', weddings (buff waistcoat)

black Oxfords

black and grey diamond-patterned silk tie or old school tie (weddings are the only time Henry wears a tie pin)

Caroline
Plain coat or jacket to go with printed dress

pearls

gloves

matching bag and shoes (one for each day of race meeting. When Caroline sets off for four days' racing, she can't see out of the back window for hats)

Jamie
Hand-me-down or jumble morning suit (harder to come by than DJ, so almost certainly doesn't fit) – charcoal, never light grey coat, light waistcoat, striped trousers

Cousin Nicholas
Number 2 dress at fellow officer's wedding, including sword ('bloody heavy') for guard of honour

Sophie
She rarely has to attend funerals – Daddy and Jamie represent the family

Weddings – one-colour silk crêpe-de-chine dress or little suit

wide-brimmed hat tilted over eyes à la Coleherne at the Royal Wedding (far trendier at best friends' weddings)

'*VrrrrOOOOOmmm—*'
as Jamie and his friends say:
'– nought to sixty in seven point four seconds.'
If you turn this page you will find yourself
    sucked in
by the whirling crankshaft,
the pounding pistons,
the zooming whizzy zappy turbo-charger
of Sloane life

Days 8 hr 28 min (av), lengthening

* Income tax payable, 1st
* New Year's Day, 1st (New Year's resolutions: Henry, less alcohol; Caroline, less ratty; Sophie, less coke; Jamie, lose virginity; Edward, be better; Emma, sing better)
* Racehorses' official birthday, 1st
* The sales
* Boat Show, Earl's Court (yoch-yochs ahoy; but it's not all Sloane. Sloanes congregate in the RYA bar)
* Twelfth Night, alias Epiphany, 6th (in Catholic countries, shops shut. In Sloaneland, Caroline takes the decorations down and lists the cards in a book which she has kept since her marriage, crossing out those who sent no card. She stacks torn-off backs of cards by the telephone for messages. Henry hates this)
* The annual planning conference (Sloane couple desires travel, certain places only considered)
* Charles I beheaded, 30th January 1649 (the service in St Mary-le-Strand draws some Sloanes even though it's RC – Sloanes like bells, smells, kings)
* British Alpine Ski Championships
* Cock shoots (pheasant shooting ends 1 February)
* Charity balls
* Rugger internationals
* Cresta Run, St Moritz (end Dec to last day Feb)
* Children back to school around 12th
* Burns Night, 25th (Scottish Sloanes eat a previously addressed haggis and try to remember all the words of 'The Immortal Memory')
* End of month: mock O-levels (as non-workers, Sloane pupils are scared witless. They now buckle down and refuse to go skiing at Easter. June is all too soon.)

The annual conference

For Sloanes away and at play

Henry and Caroline *liaise* in January – they get together to plan the year. It is their highest form of communication. They have their diaries (*Harpers & Queen* and the *Economist*). Henry has his whisky, Caroline her cup of Nes (she wants to get her way this year).
Caroline has her immutables. The first thing she writes in her diary every year is the school dates. For 1984:
Spring term 11 Jan to 29 March
    half-term 20 to 24 Feb
Summer term 24 April to 19 July
    half-term 28 May to 1 June
Autumn term 12 Sept to 14 Dec
    half-term 22 to 26 Oct
    One advantage of all one's children being Private is that their terms are all the same length. State schools have a far longer term and a far longer half-term. This makes the Science Museum safe for Sloanes for a heavenly week at the beginning of term.

Caroline's other demands are to be at *home* all May and June (garden, Season) and away August (children), and on skis sometime.
    Henry is not saying much, but come hell or high water he will be spending a week after Christmas with the Owne-Moores, if they invite him (probably leave C behind), and a week in April on the Oykel. Then skiing, then trout fishing in June, then shooting in August, not counting single days with the syndicate. It's not selfish, it's certainly not *leisure*, it's what one does. Caroline has to 'liaise nearer the time' so as not to ask people to dinner when he is mayfly fishing on the Itchen.

The party

When shall we have Our Party? (has to be hooked on to a Sloane event, eg Cricket Week). Caroline does her dinner parties in October, November and early December. A few return matches in January and February, but hunting makes you sleepy on Saturday night.

The summer holiday, Aug or Sept

Sloane Ranger families take a house or villa; just possibly a flat. Hotels are for grown-ups. They never travel First – the extra money would buy a saddle.

The choice of places is limited by prejudice. *Not* the South of France, Italian Riviera, southern Spain or Majorca, unless the villa is several kilometres inland from 'the great unwashed'. Italy: only Tuscany and Umbria in the north, Calabria in the south. Sardinia: still. Sloanes don't think they *look* rich enough to be kidnapped. One Sloanenap and all will change.

France: Britanny, the Dordogne. Portugal: the Algarve. Greece: the islands, especially Corfu and Skiathos. In Cor FU it's *always* from Corfu Villas and *always* at Nissaki; the former run by gents, the Cooksons; the latter because the hoi polloi stop at Ipsos (James Bond water motor-bikes and baked beans). Henry and Caroline boast they met Michael Heseltine in Nissaki, though they know Oxfordshire's opinion: 'The Heseltines *bought* all their furniture.'

A Sloane likes to take a villa from another Sloane: then you know it won't have horrid cushions and will have McCormick herbs in the cupboard.

If he cannot find the right thing through friends, the Sloane advertises in the *County Landowner* or the Country Gentlemen's Association magazine – *Country* – in January. CLA, 16 Belgrave Square, SW1 (235 0511); CGA, Icknield Way West, Letchworth, Herts (04626 2377). He may also place an advertisement in *The Lady*.

Caroline brings sun lotion (Ambre Solaire, or Helena Rubinstein's Golden Beauty) and dark glasses (always packs a spare pair). She sometimes sunbathes wearing nothing but the wrong make-up. Underlined on her check list is the Braun hairdryer with Continental attachment.

Caroline feels like some fun and games, but Henry has wilted in the heat.

The winter holiday, Feb or March

As Henry progresses in the occupation stakes – don't call it 'work' – he joins the winter holiday circuit. He likes it to be assumed he's been there all along.

Caroline has turned the living-room into a travel agency. At the expensive end of the gros-point stool are the chic brochures of Swan Hellenic, Serenissima and Supertravel. These frighten Henry (culcha). Luckily for him, the better culture tours are in late

---

From Caroline's Diary

The great Christmas-present changing marathon, far tougher than the sales. I wish the family would help with the lying and cheating with old carrier bags.

A spot of forward planning in January can lead to a marvellous summer with friends, sharing a villa at Nissaki on Cor FU

From Caroline's Diary

Gorgeous to be in Scotland for New Year. Lots of young came first-footing last night and today with their black bun. Pa says he prefers the English, who bring booze! Not feeling too well but no workers anywhere so first-footed the cows and helped Pa milk – the noise.
Leave kettle full and plugs in basins at night

spring and early autumn – school ties. This leaves Feb–March open for seven- or fourteen-day sun packages from such Sloane-tested firms as Kuoni, Bales, Hayes & Jarvis, Pegasus, Inter-Church, Sovereign and Thomson.

Sloane Rangers like the Caribbean (pronounced Carry be-in) and argue endlessly about the comparative merits of Antigua, St Lucia, Tobago and Barbados. Bermuda is British and Sloane – eighteenth-century houses. Sloanes are quite keen about the Far East: Bangkok and Bali especially. Caroline longs to go to the paradise island of Phuket in Thailand: Henry calls it Fuckit. Sri Lanka is growing in popularity. Kenya *was* pure Sloane – a week on photographic safari followed by a week by the sea at Mombasa or Malindi; but media coverage of poachers killing elephants has deterred that human elephant the Sloane. If you're still game, upmarket tours are run by Abercrombie & Kent. Informal family farming tours, complete with game-park trips, are organised by Tony Mills, PO Box 122, Kitale.

Sloanes also chug up and down the Nile in March in search of Agatha Christie.

The royal year

An example to us all
The Royal Year is wonderfully regular. The tours only interrupt an absolutely *clockwork progress* round the country; hence the Court Circular and a list of events booked up more than a year ahead. The Queen doesn't just look at the Supertravel bumph and say it'd be fun to go to Mustique (though her sister does). She goes *where she always goes* in a way even Sloanes have given up.

You hear wonderfully serious words in Palace circles, like 'the Court is at Windsor/Balmoral', etc. Most modern grandees can't really afford to live this way ... moving about the country, the servants in tow, *opening up* this house or that (actually the royal residences are all staffed *all* the time). This is the royal schedule and you can set your clock by it.

January: Sandringham *
February: Buckingham Palace
April: Windsor Castle *
May to mid-August: Buckingham Palace. But a week in late June/early July at Holyroodhouse, Edinburgh *
Mid-August to mid-October: Balmoral *
Mid-October to Christmas: Buckingham Palace
Christmas at Windsor accompanied by family only *
* No visits from PM, thank God

The Queen at Windsor with corgis. She'd live like a Sloane all the time if she could

Buckingham Palace (930 4832) cites the following as *really* important social occasions: Birthday Parade; State visits, opening of Parliament, garden parties; Henley Regatta; Ascot week.

'There is no longer what used to be called a season', they say stolidly.

The Queen, God bless her, wants to be slightly modern in these matters – unstuffy. The Sloane palace girls will tell you: 'The Queen likes all her houses equally ... there really isn't one she prefers over the rest ... there's no season she prefers over the rest.' Of course, if you're the Queen you *can't* admit to liking autumn best, or preferring Balmoral, or anything which might cause depression among your subjects or bad feeling in the staff and area of the least favourite house. You just forge ahead or, to use an expression the Queen would not, you go with the flow. The Queen makes a valiant effort to enjoy what's particular to each season and place (Balmoral pipers, for instance) and put up with the rest. According to Dempster, however, the Queen prefers Balmoral – mainly because it's more secluded and there aren't lorry-loads of Fleet Street hacks creeping all over the flower-beds.

From Caroline's Diary

Jamie has the beagles home for the holidays. Gorgeous little animals but hardly quiet. Sometimes I wish they had some other kennels to go to.

Snow report

Glass still going down

Though Swiss and French resorts have been echoing to Sloane whoops since mid-December, January is when low-budget Sloanes hit the Alps. Tour operators offer substantial reductions, and the weather and snow can be good. An increasingly popular way to get out is the ski coach. Most operators run several, but the top bussing company is Ski West. The coaches leave London (often, conveniently, from Gloucester Road, Heaven SW7) mid/late-Friday afternoon and arrive in Val etc about noon next day. The bunks come down at Paris and

are folded back into seats around Moutiers. The duty-free from the ferry and one's Sony Walkman make it bearable. (Videos are also starting to play a part – the real coup is Koo in a state of undress.)

Also popular with econoSloanes is self-catering flat in resorts like Tignes: good bargains in low season.

The garden and larder

Put it on the shelf

The seed catalogues come. If you are good you order immediately. If you are normal, you take a pile of catalogues skiing, bring them back unopened and order in February.

If you can bear to garden in January, spray trees and roses with tar oil. If you forget you don't fret – it gives the blackspot a fighting chance.

Flowers and plants every Sloane has

Violas, pansies (usually blue or white, never mixed, to underplant the roses); pinks; button daisies; Canterbury bells; clematis (CLEMatis); rosemary; hostas (*very* Sloane – and *very* sluggy); hebes; potentillas; doronicum (for spring); delphiniums; lilies; peonies; phlox; irises; Japanese anemones; verbascum;

From Caroline's Diary

All back to school, including beagles. Sad.

Cheered up by helping Elizabeth with Annabel's wedding. So much to do before June. A wedding and a season seem a bit much for the poor old mums. Booked the church and helped her measure the lawn for marquee sites.

January

alchemilla mollis (lady's mantle, for flower arrangements: conveniently grows in shade); astilbes, if the ground is moist enough; sedums, in variety; anthemis; honeysuckle; lavender (a lavender hedge is as good as a nursery fender).

Roses

On and on Sloanes go about these. Avoid most hybrid teas – *terribly* vulgar. Go for old-fashioned shrub roses and floribundas. *Favourites*: Iceberg, Buff Beauty, Penelope, Felicia, Cornelia. Old Blush China and Rosa mundi make good hedges. *Ramblers*: Albertine, Paul's Scarlet, Goldfinch, Zéphyrine Drouhin ('the rose without a thorn') for climbing walls, Mme Alfred Carrier and Kiftsgate for climbing trees (and weighing down buildings – Kiftsgate climbs to 90 feet). *Damask roses*: like Mme Hardy which grows into a six-foot bush. Old *moss roses* make the Sloane heart ache for the good old days – before they were born.

Larder and freezer

Henry is jealous of the deep-freeze. Caroline is still in love with it, because Sloanes belong to the plan-ahead classes. They hate dining in *fashionable* houses where the hostess cooks while they wait for *hours*. 'We were *starving*. Henry was complEEtli pissed by the time she produced postage stamps of gourbloody novelle.'

After the children have gone back to school, Caroline cracks into making the annual 30, 40, 50, even 70 lb of marmalade as soon as the Sevilles appear. She goes to bed murmurlading to Henry about job satisfaction.

Young lads and old birds

The boys' shoot

Though the pheasant season starts officially in October and Sloanes shoulder their guns a month later, it is not until January that Sloane fathers

A Father's Advice to His Son

If a sportsman true you'd be,
Listen carefully to me.

Never, never let your gun
Pointed be at anyone;
That it may unloaded be
Matters not the least to me.

When a hedge or fence you cross,
Though of time it cause a loss,
From your gun the cartridge take,
For the greater safety's sake.

If 'twixt you and neighbouring gun
Birds may fly or beasts may run,
Let this maxim e'er be thine:
FOLLOW NOT ACROSS THE LINE.

Stops and beaters oft unseen
Lurk behind some leafy screen;
Calm and steady always be:
NEVER SHOOT WHERE YOU CAN'T SEE.

Keep your place and silent be:
Game can hear and game can see;
Don't be greedy, better spared
Is a pheasant than one shared.

You may kill or you may miss,
But at all times think of this:
All the pheasants ever bred
Won't repay for one man dead.

COMMANDER MARK BEAUFOY, 1920s

organise a boys' pheasant shoot, to round off the Christmas holidays. Young Sloanes often are given the poem 'Never, never let your gun . . .', which they learn by heart. It's never too early to know that peasants could be lurking behind some leafy screen, but as for 'better spared is a pheasant than one shared' – half the Henrys who are bad shots have their pride saved by feeling they shot a *bit* of that bird. (A good shot always has such a big score that he can humour the hopeless Henry on his left.)

If the young Sloane's father has a shoot, he might take his place in the line at 11, with an empty .410 for a year or two. At 13 he is given a loaded 20-bore, and by 17, a 16-bore, and perhaps a leather-bound game-book as a confirmation present (a confirmed killer). It is now time to have his own first shoot.

You ask about ten boys – Henry insists on invitations for all the big local land-owners' sons, no matter how odious. The keeper has stuck a line of numbered pegs in the ground in the wood as for a grown-ups' shoot, and Jamie borrows Henry's initialled case for the boys to draw their numbers from. Henry gives a final lecture. Sloanes are the last safe shots, keeping all the rules – while

Jamie, his 12-bore and the old bore in his plus-fours

keepers, foreigners and noovos relax and live dangerously. Keepers are quite proud of their war wounds, the little black dots beneath the skin pumped into them by an over-enthusiastic foreign gun.

No such fun on a boys' shoot. They are completely correct. After each drive they say to each other 'Any joy?' 'A little joy.' Jamie *doesn't* say he fired five shots and didn't hit anything. Everyone knows how everyone else is doing.

If you need to ask how much a cartridge costs, you can't afford it. (It's 7p.) Smart shooting Sloanes buy them in bulk from ICI, forming a syndicate to do it and flogging them off to friends, 10,000 a time for a keen killer.

At the end of the day, each boy receives a brace from the keeper, at the same time as handing him a fiver, and writes a thank-you letter afterwards to Henry.

The cock shoot

The pheasant season (ends 1 February) is brought to a close by one – or possibly two – 'cocks only' days, to mop up the males. Hens must be left for breeding. One woman landowner (rich, not Sloane) had a cock shoot of eight guns, all of them former lovers. Cock-shooting is not for duffers – the pheasants are

Game ☆ Stroganoff

The freezer is literally stuffed with game by the end of the shooting season. Space will soon have to be found for Henry's salmon, so with the New Year Caroline makes an extravagant dish that uses up plenty of pheasants and wild duck.

For 8–10

2 pheasants ● 3 wild duck ● ½ lb mushrooms ● 1 large onion ● ½ pint sour cream ● 1 orange ● 2½ oz butter ● 1½ oz flour ● ¾ pint game stock ● salt and pepper

Roast the birds in a very hot oven for 10 minutes.

Remove the breasts and thighs only and skin them. Cut the meat into pencil-thick, 1½-inch long strips. Use the remains for soup or pâté and make the bones into stock. Grate the orange rind – or better, if you have an orange zester, make thin strips of peel. Slice the mushrooms and onion finely. Blanch the onion and orange peel strips for 2–3 minutes in boiling salted water, then strain and drain well. Sauté the mushrooms in the butter, briefly. Add the meat, orange peel and onion. Add the flour and mix it in well. Add the stock and stir till it thickens nicely. Taste for seasoning. Add the sour cream and whizzle it all around to melt the dollops, but don't let it boil.

Serve with plain rice and a green veg like broccoli.

January

Caroline to
Zara Kimbolton-Smith

fewer, flying higher, and you have to judge their sex in the air.

The gun dogs (labradors, setters, spaniels) have become quite good by now. Training and handling these is a sport for female Sloane wrinklies. At one particularly grand shoot, the guests were assembled in the drawing-room before lunch when the hostess, a keen dog-handler, came hurrying in saying 'I'm so sorry to have kept you waiting. I've been searching *high and low* for Dominic's cock.'

The sales

Pull in the sheets

Sales fit Sloanes like a hunting boot. Henrietta Tavistock is one of the avid first-day punters at Harvey Nicks in Knightsbridge, dressed in navy blue Husky and no doubt looking for more navy blue. Sloanes want the best in the same design at the same price as last year. They also want to stock up on wedding presents. Some other, younger Sloanes have temporary jobs behind the counter. It's nice to go to these fresh-faced shops – Simpson's, the Scotch

Don't stand too close: she kicks

House, Burberrys, Lillywhites, Maxwell Croft, Harvey Nichols, Jaeger (some Sloanes get their entire wardrobe in the Jaeger sale), Liberty's (for fabrics and children's clothes), Pedro Jonez (Peter Jones), for china, sheets etc, Colefax & Fowler Chintz Shop: Not Harrods unless you have tinies – a normal person can't fight her way in any more for the TV crews.

A young male Sloane was manning the lift at Simpson's when a woman asked for cruisewear. 'What are you looking for, Madam?' 'Bathing suits.' 'I wouldn't bother if I were you – there isn't much left.' Alas, also in the lift was a woman director of the store, and he was fired quicker than you can say 'Salesmanship hit a rock.' The drawback about Sloanes is that they know their first duty is to their fellows, not the corporate image.

Oxfam is seen by Sloanes as a permanent sale of classics. 'Oxfam' is the English gentlewoman's answer to 'Who's your dressmaker?' As a crumbly Sloane aunt said: 'Don't know about all this modern nonsense about fancy underwear. Personally I always wear William's.'

Dearest 2

I don't think I was cut out for motherhood. I try hard to follow your 'No tension' rule, but the bar seems to open a little earlier each evening and I know that after one or two my militant tendency takes over. Henry keeps out of my way – even more annoying.

Let's meet in London ASAP, re winter holiday plans and yr news – does he still charm and amuse you? How about F & M Thurs 11 am? I'll be there, in see-but-not-seen corner, unless you ring.

Lots of love.
Caro xxx.

PS *How do you make dumplings? Henry wants them for next shooting lunch. Will Fortnum's have them in tins – or frozen??!*

The teenage special year
Young life is a ball

There's a new sub-group of teen-to-twenties balls which are being invaded by more and more *really* young groovers, which makes the ones in their twenties feel absolutely *ancient*. You find yourself sitting next to a sophisticated member of the opposite sex, but when you ask them what they do, they say they're at school. You ask: 'Do you teach?' and they say no, they're still at school; you twig and say: 'Are you doing Oxbridge?' – 'No' – 'A-levels?' – 'No' – and finally you realise they're fourteen.

You get sent bumph about the latest ball by a friend on the committee. The Junior Committee, a lovely new formalism, consists of at least 20 young people selected for their far-reaching, grand and moneyed set of acquaintances. You decide to get a party together, ask friends and make them pay by cheque in advance. Inexperienced party-organisers send off large cheques themselves, and unscrupulous friends of friends who were roped in to make up numbers don't cough up.

If you're going to dinner at the ball, numbers are about eight or ten – this is because it's virtually impossible to dig up more than five men who will pay the full price of dinner tickets. But if you're going after dinner, then you may have up to 20 people – the more the merrier – and go out to dinner, or else have a DP (dinner party) at the organiser's flat/house. All the girls help – they bring quiche, cheese, French bread, salad, etc; all the quichés . . . men bring bottles.

Finding an interesting and inspired venue is tricky. Plushy hotels are boring. A Horror Ball was held in the Chamber of Horrors, but the little horrors started removing limbs from gruesome murderers; no more parties *there*. Somewhere like Hammersmith Palais is best – shabby and befitting the new age of decadence.

January

Big bashes

JANUARY

Blizzard Greater London Fund for the Blind (262 0191), Hilton. 15–21s – winter equivalent of the Heatwave. Emma thinks she's arrived – it's like a real grown-up ball.

Bluebird NSPCC (580 8812), Hyde Park Hotel. 16s and over, but Emma infuriates her elder brother and sister by getting in too. It usually ends in tears (mostly from mothers on sight of their darlings in the bitingly candid pages of *Ritz* or *Tatler* – Emma's strapless top pulled down to the waist, Edward roaring drunk with a joint hanging out of his mouth . . .).

Peacock KIDS (969 2817), Royal Lancaster Hotel. 16–25s.

APRIL

Black and White ICAA (730 9891), Café Royal (date not fixed). Some oldies but more Emma's and Sophie's age-group. Very popular. Fewer people bother about dressing b&w – more try to startle by being different (so nobody startles in the end).

Rollerball (624 7612). In search of a venue. Banned from the Café Royal and Rainbow Suite because there were so many gatecrashers. OTT Baby Legsers, no one in black tie. Rock 'n' roll dancing, including an elimination dance in which Jamie manages to look cool by standing in roughly the same spot, showing off his nifty arm movements, while Sophie is thrown in a dizzy twirl to all corners of the floor. Non-SRs win and Jamie grumbles that it was Sophie's fault *they* didn't. Grotty cold buffet, sweaty disco.

MARCH

Oyster GAP Activity Projects (Reading 872869), Whitbread Brewery.

JULY

Heatwave Greater London Fund for the Blind (262 0191), Hilton. 15–21s. Emma swings the night away with groovy gangs of school pals.

Masquerade Save the Children Fund (703 5400), Hurlingham. Compulsory masks. Last year's band was Naked Lunch.

SEPTEMBER

Ceroc Nansen International Children's Centre (James Cronin, 235 7822), Hammersmith Palais. Flouncy minis still – they swirl round so sexily – long brown legs, baggy lacy socks and plimsolls. French rock 'n' roll. Stamina needed. Trendy and good fun.

Bouncing Queen Charlotte's Special Care Baby Unit (Lorraine Seaward, 351 4333), Windsor Safari Park. In 1982, 1200 hooligans ripped the Commonwealth Institute to pieces. 1983 found

them in their natural habitat (dress safari). Cheapie tickets, barbeque and breakfast.

DECEMBER

Bobbin Royal School of Needlework (727 4330), Madame Tussaud's. 16–21s. Glassy-eyed expressions, mixing with the greats.

Cinderella NSPCC (580 8812), Dorchester. All ages, but predominantly young and debby. Some dress as Cinders – ribbons in hair, tattered frocks, white-stockinged legs, pumps.

Crystal ICAA (730 9891), Savoy. 14–18s. Emma goes, but Sophie wouldn't be seen dead there as all the boys are *so* juvenile.

Feathers Feathers Clubs Association (723 9167), Hammersmith Palais. 'What an enlightened committee' think the Sloanes – such a groovy venue. Inspires wicked behaviour, including parent-shocking horizontal embraces.

Metallic Queen Elizabeth's Foundation for the Disabled (Louise Foottit, 831 9001), Glaziers' Hall. Everyone dressed in gold, silver, tin foil, lurex, glitter, tinsel – even shimmering swimsuits.

University clubs and their annual events

CAMBRIDGE

Athenaeum. About 20 members; pink and white striped tie. Cottenham point-to-point, Mar; clay pigeon shoot vs. Oxford, Mar.

Pitt, Jesus Lane. Own premises, like a London club, but has seen better days. Open to anyone but need 15 votes in your favour. Cheapish lunch and dinner; cocktails on Monday.

Food and Wine Society. Dons and undergraduates hold dinners with the very best food and wine they can muster – for budding Foodies.

Terrapins. Ten chic-est women in Cambridge. Termly drinks and dinners; women run the evening. Some SRMs can't take the role-reversal.

Wylie. Notorious – everyone gets *so* seriously drunk that the club's future is on sticky ground.

Also: *Parnell, Hawks* (sporting blues).

Balls (see p 71)

OXFORD

Gridiron, known as the Grid. 100–130 members pretending to be grown-up (reading *Telegraph* over school-style lunch and champagne).

Bullingdon, a.k.a. the Buller. Turquoise and gold tails and ties, mostly Eton SRs who never got into Pop. Snobbish, rich and drunken with hunky sex appeal (official Bullingdon girls have to have slept with five members). Notorious point-to-point, February, preceded by the Bullingdon (liquid) Breakfast, preceded by the Beagle Ball (club members zombie-like and near to death by late afternoon at the p-to-p).

Assassins. Many of the same members as the Buller. Achieved fame after the 1982 Thatcher's Hotel Incident in Thame. Termly drinks parties, usually fancy dress (recent theme: Un-Thamed – plenty of Incredible Hunks and gorillas).

Piers Gaveston. A shade too camp for Hoorays, although they enjoy the debauchery. One ball a year, normally at Christmas in Oxford, but last year's was a huge dampish squib at the Café Royal in May.

George. Formerly all-female, now mixed (doesn't appeal to SRMs, who like chaps-only clubbing).

Dangerous Sports. All the fun of racing down a black run at St Moritz on anything but skis (eg a grand piano) or being shot from a cannon (*Going For It*) *and* getting drunk afterwards. Mostly ex-Oxford participants – students can't afford it.

Also: *Keats, Kingsley* (Worcester), *Allendale* (Balliol), *Loder* (Christ Church), *Vincent's* (sporting blues).

Balls (see p 71)

BRISTOL

Beano. Red and black bow-ties. Dine in private rooms. Champagne breakfasts with ladies (decorative). Drinks party plus dancing, St Patrick's Day (17 March). Moderate debauchery (standing on tables and removing trousers).

EXETER

Genghis Khan dining club. Termly dinners. Predominantly old Radleians who wish they were at Oxford.

Parties:

Sanctuary, June, held by residents of the smart Sanctuary house after exams.

Copperwalls, June, similar to the above.

Prince Charles's sporting tour

The Sloane as sponge

Sloanes who are keen on sport have to flatter and cadge, in a gentlemanly way. Outside every fat estate is a pack of thin Sloanes trying to get in. A Sloane with good shooting is pleased to invite a Sloane with good stalking, but the unlanded Sloanes are much less attractive, weedily offering their firm's opera box and the fact they cast/shoot/ride straight – sometimes.

Even the most landed Sloane, Prince Charles, has not got everything. His parents do not live in good hunting country and have no fishing river, except the Dee at Balmoral. Prince Charles goes up to the Helmsdale in the spring, end March/April, and gets cross because the chum he goes with always catches more than he does. He likes fishing in Iceland in August with Lord and Lady Tryon.

Prince Charles (HRH to his fellow sportsmen) actually spends months a year at killer sports. He is a kind man, but he has the Sloane view of death. He was careful to site himself at Highgrove, within reach of four hunts – the Beaufort, the Berkeley, the Cotswold and the Heythrop – but four are not enough. HRH gallops the length and breadth of the country in search of greener fields and a redder fox.

His practice is to ask the Master whether a hunt would like to give him a

'We were doing a ton down the M4, Camilla was shooting *enormous* tigers (*ruined* the paintwork) and I'd just about mastered her bra strap when we flew off the road . . .'

'Off! Off! Off! Off!'

day's sport. Instantly, all the gates are opened, literally, and all the wire removed. The honoured Master makes a falsely brilliant display, pulling in the best bits of the Saturday country and the best bits of the Wednesday country and any nice coverts he had been saving for a foxless day. Prince Charles arrives with his hunting equerry. HRH wears a cap, whether a hunt's rule is top hats or no top hats. The royal head must not be bashed in before the crown.

The field are all thrilled to their boots, especially the women. 'Where else would you talk to Him as naturally as I'm talking to you now?'

Exception that proves the ruler

Last year after Christmas the Prince was staying in the north for a week and wanted to get in as many days hunting as possible. He made the usual request to the neighbouring hunt, but the unusual answer was No. 'I'm as happy to have him to hunt as the next man,' said the person responsible, 'but we'd disappoint the loyal followers on Saturday if we let HRH hunt on Friday.'

Such loyalty to followers is good, but it was a bad move in the sport-swapping game. This person may like stalking or shooting, but he won't be going to Balmoral any moor.

Prince Charles out with the Cheshire. He keeps *dozens* of hunts happy

Footpath

THE AQUARIUS SLOANE

January 21st, enter the Aquarius Sloane

The Aquarian Sloane is an exception to the Sloane rule. Charismatic and magnetic, your personality defies analysis. With that and your sensous voice, no one seems to notice that you're hardly a stunning physical specimen. But then, with your assets, who needs to be?

Your life is absolutely teeming with friends – or is it just teeming? To you, people are like books – you don't always want to read the same one. In fact, you like reading about ten at once.

You're really a bit of a non-conformist – like reading the *Guardian* at the office. You're not a slave to the Salt Mine, but that doesn't mean you're afraid of hard work.

As for romance, you're really happiest with a 'chum' – or several 'chums'. Someone you can *talk* to – bed and restaurants are not really your scene. And children – they're rum little creatures. But one *has* to have them. Nanny's one of your few worthwhile extravagances.

One of the reasons people like you is that your charm seems effortless – you never seem to compete. Not for you the snide remark, the put-down. You just drift on if places or persons don't suit.

Your secret: Your secrets are your own.

On Henry's mind

● Telephone Turnbull & Asser (01-930 0502) for date of their suit and overcoat sale.
● Work out by how much to increase insurance policies, and renew (including contents of Caroline's freezer).
● Renew subscriptions. This is the horrendous side of January. (There's *Brooks's*, about £300 – though worth it for the reciprocal memberships, especially the Knickerbocker on Central Park for $45 a night. The *Turf*, about £250. The *Royal Ocean Racing Club*, £35, useful when crewing for the boss. The nightclub, *Annabel's*, £150. The lunching club in the City, *Stags*, £50 – the firm pays for the other, really pompous lunching club. The *Lansdowne*, £60 a couple plus £25 entrance fee for London members; £20 plus £25 for country members – for shopping Caroline down from the country or Sophie with friends after work. *Country Gentlemen's Association*, £12; *Country Landowners' Association*, £s in ratio to acreage; *National Trust*, £25 for

the family. *Friends of Covent Garden*, £18.) That's over £900 already, and you know you've forgotten a few.
● Stock Exchange joke: *'What's the difference between herpes and Brit Oil? You've got some chance of getting rid of the first.'*

Forward planning

★ Book British Rail ferry for Cowes Week if you want to take the car (Portsmouth 2744).
★ Last chance to apply for Wimbledon tickets (p 74). If you can stand paying another subscription, all members of the Lawn Tennis Association (£10 a year, plus £5 to join) get a special allocation of Wimbledon tickets – after all, you may fail in the ballot.
★ Book on the Grand National train (p 40).
★ Apply for Ascot (p 70).
★ Advertise for a villa for August.

FEBRUARY

Snow report

Switzerland, Austria: conditions good
Sloane skiers have finally realised that France is out for the three weeks after the first Saturday in February – the French school holidays. So this month becomes high season in Verbier and other Swiss resorts, and in Zürs, Lech, St Anton and other Austrian resorts. St Moritz has jet-set SRs – for the Cresta.

Only smoothies go to Gstaad, the Opulent People's place. The Palace nightclub is like a giant bed of watercress full of famous faces. C'est magnifique, mais ce n'est pas Sloane.

Caroline and exercise

Keeping up the (muscle) tone
At the beginning of February, Caroline shapes up for an early summer of flat tummy and tiny bikini (it *makes* you seem so much thinner than those smart one-piece suits – the principle of divide and fool), but really exercise and doing yourself up generally present a conundrum to Sloanes. They believe in one part of it – the practical sweaty ritual part, and making an effort – and they like to get caught up in a popular thing sometimes. But they do *not* like the grim-dedication-to-the-self side at all.

The aunt-who-always-gives-v-good presents came through with the Jane Fonda tome last Christmas. Caroline is excited since *everyone* has got it and is flinging themselves around the room. Hong Kong SRs are *especially* excited – it's the arm exercises. You can't have flabby arms on the junk, looking like old hens' throats, especially with all the new female talent that pours into HK on every plane.

Caroline has to admit that she *does* feel better for her aerobics – though they don't come easily. The only exercise that does is the buttock lifts – accustomed as she is to the missionary position. But she tries 'to do some' every morning – though during the school holidays, the children fall about laughing (and Henry is worried to see her tits contracting). Besides, Henry is not sure about Mzzzz Fonda's politics.

Joke as they might, 'Where do you dance/exercise?' is a standard SR question, a regular dinner-party topic. Henry is 'rather riveted', and longs to go and watch. Caroline doubts his motives.

Exercise classes

Caroline will go to one of the following London places:

LOTTE BERK ('Good old Lotte, she started it all anyway'), 465 Fulham Road, SW6 and 29 Manchester Street, W1 (935 8905).

SUSIE BOWER, at the Duke of York's HQ, King's Road, SW3 (373 4082). You need a pass to get in ('But you can't use it to shop in Peter Jones'), there are always terrific security checks. Music ranges from Handel to the Stranglers (Susie's Wykehamist sons help her choose modern music: she is an ex-model and journalist, and 'absolutely *fantastic*').

JILLI FORTESCUE, 35 Surrey Lane, SW11 (228 8416). A slow form of Jane Fonda (though Jilli Fortescue has been doing it *far* longer: she was with Granny's and started on her own years ago). Work to the sound of Jilli's voice. Small classes, all friends. £3 per hour.

BODY'S (Jane Birkbeck), 250 King's Road, SW3 (351 5686) is for Mayfair Mercs, or Supersloanes, and so expensive.

PINEAPPLE DANCE STUDIO, 7 Langley Street, WC2 (836 4004). Good value. Caro goes with a girlfriend, as Covent Garden isn't really her beat. But loves mixing with all sorts.

Massage

Ex-estate agent Sloane Jeremy Glyn massages at GRAFTON'S HEALTH STUDIO, Belmont Hall, 27a Belmont Close, SW4 (720 2895) for £15 an hour, or will visit you (736 3491).

Self-defence

James Bond stuntman Doug Robinson teaches you how to defend yourself with a rolled H & Q, plus the keys to your Renault 5 and the heels on your Guccis. BOJANGLES STUDIO, Royal Ascot Squash Club, High Street, Ascot, Berks (0990 28312).

Point-to-points

Amateur Lad wins again

First Saturday in February to second in June

Point-to-pointing (Peter-peeing) is out-and-out Sloane because it's got picnic baskets (Sloanes are the hamper classes); it's connected with hunting (horses have to have been 'regularly and fairly' hunted); it's amateurs only, and it is usually so muddy and cold before May no sane person would want to go.

Only the keen *do* go, in February. But

Sane people watch from above hooligan-level at the Bullingdon point-to-point

on a Saturday afternoon in late March, or in April or May, with the leaves new, the sun out, and some young bowler-hatted duchess galloping past in the Buchanan Whisky race, a point-to-point is really the place to be.

The Buchanan races, at the start of the card, are a return to the old meaning of point-to-point – from landmark to landmark across country. Eighteenth-century gentlemen took steeples as their points, and this custom begat twins, steeplechasing (permanent courses, National Hunt rules) and point-to-pointing (ad hoc courses, but some are permanent now).

Up and over

Point-to-point jumps are six inches lower than steeplechase jumps and the riders are bigger. The pointers carry 12 stone 7 for men, 11 for women, and before the season a lot of hunting people and Army officers try to crash-diet.

At the first jump, several fall off their tiny saddles, and a mass of loose horses, galloping on at the head of the field, cause more falls and thoroughly confuse Betting Henry. His cousin Hooray

BRILLAT SAVARIN'S FONDUE

For 4

4 eggs • ⅓ of their weight in grated Gruyère – but Cheddar will do (say 2⅔ oz) • ⅙ of the weight of the cheese in butter (say just under 1 oz) • salt • freshly-ground black pepper

Back from skiing, everyone misses the fondues. Caroline has tried making them at home, but they never seem to taste as good here as they did in Méribel. This is not quite a fondue, but it's a delicious eggy-buttery-cheesy dish with a hint of the fonduest memories. It's a good standby for a late bite after the theatre or cinema.

Break the eggs into a basin and beat them well. Add the cheese and the butter, cut into little bits. Stir well, then cook the mixture in a small saucepan, stirring constantly until the mixture thickens. Add salt and pepper to taste. Don't let the thing boil or it will be horrible.

Serve it, like Mrs Beeton suggests, on a very hot silver plate and drink burgundy with it.

Henry adds to the melée: Hoorays come in droves to point-to-points and spend the afternoon (thank God) in the beer tent. As the annual bible of the sport, *Horse and Hound's Hunter Chasers and Point-to-Pointers* says, 'Every year he (the announcer) assures us that the public address will not be made available for personal messages and every year the public is regaled with pleas from one drunk to meet another at the beer tent or for Jeremy to return to the car because Daddy wants to go home.'

Amateur races are called bumpers, because all the jockeys bump up and down in the saddle. Bad horses, bad jockeys and a bad course is a recipe for a bad accident, and there are fatalities. When one Sloane woman was carted off to hospital with a mangled pelvis, her husband Henry (MFH, of course) abandoned his judge's bowler and rode in the next two races.

The sport is disorganised, and often worse. At an Army lightweight race at Tweseldown in 1981, an unauthorised runner suddenly appeared from behind the bushes and made for the first fence. He was stopped there, however, by three refusals, and disappeared again into the bushes. It turned out he was a Scots Guards officer who had tried to enter for the race after entries closed and decided to compete anyway. The Jockey Club fined him £100.

The prizes are tiny – around £50 (a maximum of £150 for all three places in the race). The event is held to raise money for the local hunt. The Jockey Club won't let hunts charge the spectator for admission, so they charge for car-parking on the course (£2 to £10) and the race card (so ten giddy Sloanes share the race card of an eleventh who is *trying* to study form. Sloanes are similarly tight with theatre programmes).

There are usually six races, including a Men's Open and a Ladies' Open. The Ladies' race tends to hold the course speed record (lighter riders).

A kick from the boot

But for normal Sloanes, the point about point-to-points is what Americans call tailgate culture – your picnic (see p 34, A/B – not *all* liquid), shared with any friends who pass. 'Henry likes quiche and he's a real man.' Herpes-conscious punters circulate with their own plastic mugs.

Supersloanes have Sloanemobiles – cars fitted with a platform on the roof and a metal ladder to get a good view. And they bring a portable telly for the Saturday afternoon triple sportswatch beloved of Sloanes: rugger from Twickers and flat-racing on the box, your point-to-pointing friends on the field. Henry discovers that the cigarette-lighter attachment doesn't work and

Bar P-To-P·

non *gravitas* sed *gravity*

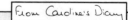

From Caroline's Diary

Pa to the Perth bull sales; glad he went or he wouldn't see anyone from the end of shooting to the reopening of the dining-room in May. He can't hear the telephone from his telly cocoon.

stuffs the leads in the battery terminals, which guarantees a push-start later. Sometimes a semi-Sloane brother (a pimply) tries to watch the Saturday film. The Sloanes push him off the Sloanemobile.

The riders are terribly attractive, tall and thin (none of the little monkey types). They ride in their owners' 'colours' (jerseys or silks). The watchers, in kit A – dull browns and greens – are like hen birds watching their cocks.

Young Sophies set up their own cocktail party with the YOs (young officers) beside the beer tent, well away from the parents' car. They don't watch the racing – good thing, they'd scare the horses. Lots of 'Air hellairs' and doffed trilby or cap, kiss on either cheek.

Keen Sloanes know to arrive half an hour before the first race and leave before the last. (Though I've-only-come-for-the picnic Sloanes arrive in the middle of the first race and talk the car park stewards into letting them usurp the

Cirencester Hoorays at the Beaufort point-to-point

reserved spot of another late arrival who thinks he's safe.) But you always find a bottleneck at the gate. Sophie, in her Golf, is spinning her wheels furiously (handbrake on), throwing mud into the faces of the YOs who are trying to push her. Rollses are regularly removed by tractor.

Sloane meets horse

Before setting out, if it's frosty or raining, ring up to see if it's still on (number in the *Horse and Hound* book). The p-to-p calendar is given in *Horse and Hound* at the end of January, and the day's fixtures are in *Sporting Life*, but the whole thing may be called off at 7.30 am, after you've condensed all the food in the house into a picnic and invited a Sloanemobileful of extreme rowdies.

These meetings are Sloane. In chronological order:

TWESELDOWN, 7 meetings. Staff College & RMA Sandhurst Drag opens the p-to-p season. Very Army scene (3 miles from Aldershot), but not

Army-owned any more (bought by Sloane family, the Bullens). Clubhouse with warm lavatories if you belong.

LARKHILL. 6 meetings, starting with United Services in Feb. Owned by the Army. Siberian winds over Salisbury plain.

THE BULLINGDON, Kingston Blount, Feb. The dreaded blue-bow-tied Hooray Henrys of the Bullingdon club (who *never* watch a race) have behaved so badly over the years that their point-to-point has been banned and now hides under the name Oxford University Hunt Club. But they still drink all afternoon and fall over. Lunch in the Cherry Tree pub, if not picnic.

CAMBRIDGE UNIVERSITY UNITED HUNTS (The Drag), Cottenham, Feb. The Cambridge equivalent of the Bullingdon, but more students watch because more ride in it. Cottenham p-to-p cake is locally famous: two layers of fruit cake sandwiched together with vanilla butter-cream and dusted with sugar.

THE BEAUFORT, Didmarton, March. Smart. Princess Michael of Kent rode in the Buchanan old-fashioned race in 1983. The point about expensive hunts is that the horses are better.

GARTHORPE, 4 meetings, March to May. All very expensive hunts: Cottesmore, Belvoir, Quorn, Melton Hunt Club (May) which has the final of the Albright & Wilson national ladies' championships.

THE PEGASUS AND KING'S TROOP RHA, Kimble, March. The Bar p-to-p. Watch barristers obey the law of gravity.

THE COWDRAY at Midhurst, the OLD BERKS at Lockinge. Both Easter Monday. Pineapples start their point-to-point season at Easter. There are 16 p-to-ps on Easter Monday and you *should be at one*. Sussex Sloanes wonder which of the two: perhaps Lockinge just gets its nose in front.

THE HEYTHROP, Chipping Norton, midweek meeting in April. Sponsored by the National Westminster Bank. Fine new course in the Cotswolds. Sloanest of all p-to-ps – even the car park stewards are gentlemen. 4-mile men's open for Lord Ashton of Hyde's cup: most p-to-p races are 3 miles. And an Old Etonian and Old Harrovian race.

CHADDESLEY CORBETT, 4 meetings. The Lady Dudley cup at the Worcestershire in April is the Cheltenham Gold Cup of point-to-pointing: 3¼ miles.

FIFE, late April or early May. The most social Scottish Peter-pee.

MIDDLETON, Whitwell-on-the-Hill, Yorkshire, May. 4½-mile men's open for Lord Grimthorpe's gold cup is the Grand National of p-to-ps. The ladies' open is 4 miles.

MARYLAND HUNT CUP, America, April. The Sloanes' cousins the preppies all go to their equivalent of a point-to-point-cum-Grand National, the relentlessly amateur (no betting) Maryland Hunt Cup, over HUGE timber jumps. The horses wear rubber leg-protectors. Two winners of the MHC have subsequently won at Aintree. But tailgate first.

In terms of the ability of the horses (variable) and their riders (*unbelievably* variable), point-to-pointing is the only betting sport in which Sloanes know far more than the bookies. It is not uncommon to see schoolgirls and boys tucking away a big roll of money at the end of the day.

The covering season – horses

The race is not always to the swift nor the National to the strong, but that's the way to bet

15 February to 15 July

Horses, the opium of the Sloanes, take up a huge amount of Henry's time, money and brainpower. He wouldn't eat horsemeat, because it's the sacred animal. The horse is restless, physical, fast, strong, and above all competitive – he *likes* winning. And without being accused of 'side' a horse can be as forward and pushy and arrogant as it likes. Sloanes transfer all their suppressed longings and vulgarities on to the horse without even having heard of Kraft-Ebbing.

Horse-covering sets the tone for all other sorts of covering in the Sloane mind. In the spring, the longer days bring the maiden and barren mares into season (barren means not pregnant that year).

Thoroughbred horses all have the same *official* birthday, 1 January. The gestation period is eleven months. The trick for breeders is to time the foaling right. It is an advantage for a two-year-old or three-year-old to be as old and strong as possible when racing against others the same age on paper. A foal born in mid-January is perfect. But a foal born in December is *disastrous*, a year old at a few weeks. (In a small remote stud it could possibly be kept hidden until the right date, but tongues wag in a multimillion-pound industry.)

The Jockey Club suggests the 15th as a safe day to begin covering, but some sentimental stud-owners start on 14th because it's St Valentine's day.

When Shergar was horsenapped, all his ♂♂♂'s worth £○○○s went up in sm○○○ke

Breeding business

A stallion stands at such-and-such a stud and the mares are brought to him. He does three coverings a day. As a racehorse he was owned by one rich owner – or by four people or so – but a top-class stallion is usually divided into 40 parts by a syndicate. (A lucky trainer or stud director has 50 horses and four owners but an unlucky one has 50 horses and 200 owners.) The owners are the worst thing about racing – they ring up, they turn up and they drink. (200×4 large Scotches=£a lot.)

The shareholders in a stallion can send their mares to him: their money buys an annual nomination (on the basis of 40 coverings a season). There's gold in them thar haunches. A $\frac{1}{40}$ share of Shergar's potential stud career cost

$$£\frac{8m}{40} = £200,000,$$

and the stud fee for Be My Guest is £75,000, whether a foal results or not. In many cases the fee is split: 50 per cent for the nomination and 50 per cent when the mare is certified in foal. If you haven't a mare to send to him one year you can always sell the nomination, for perhaps £50,000 and upward if the progeny are proving successful.

An owner may retire a horse to stud smartly after he's done well as a three-year-old, in case of being exposed as the best in a bad year. Henry tut tuts at this, because a horse doesn't fully develop until five. Some of the greatest horses, however (Red Rum, Brown Jack), couldn't go to stud because they're geldings. Why geld a horse that might be good, Caroline asks? She is a) pleased, b) shocked by the answer: a), an entire horse (pronounced ENtire) tends to be excitable and uncontrollable; b), he may masturbate and take the edge off his

---

From Caroline's Diary

Helping Eliz with Annabel's wedding. So unlike our day when we fought Ma and Pa to let us do it quietly. Annabel wants more BMs and pages, Walesier dress, grander firms every second. After stormy family session, decided to combine the after-wedding dance and Sophie's coming out. My loud voice and clear mind have their uses. Will give Lifeboat party before marquee goes back – 3rd bird with one stone. Cancelled the Orangery.

The wedding list strictly 400 because John doesn't want to buy any more champagne, having organised it all ten years ago – tempting providence, says Sophie. 'Can't we have 250 people, because it's our champagne?' says Annabel. At least Simon's seen her as she is.

Ordered the invitations for wedding and dance. They take 4 weeks and have to go out 2 months early. Booked caterers. Sarah Arche-Ryvell wanted them for same date. Phew.

Eliz heard from PeterTownend saying 'I'm so thrilled to hear about your lovely daughter's engagement and am very much looking forward to her wedding'!! Cheek! – except Annabel wants to be in the Tatler. She's being photographed by Rosalind Mann so she'll be in Country Life. I said Betty Kenward is who matters.

form just before the big race. Horses are so designed that they can reach their own extremities with their mouths. (At least, this is what Henry says.)

Good breeding

The actual moment of covering is unimpressive. After the mare has been tested by a 'teaser stallion' and found willing, the teaser is taken away and the real stallion brought. The mare's boots have been put on (to protect the stallion from a kick in a vital spot). The stallion, operational part dangling rather awkwardly like a long Christmas stocking,

jumps up on the mare from behind and grips her withers with his teeth for a few minutes. *Nothing appears to be happening.* He slips down off her, the stocking loosely splayed and gaping now at the end like an elephant's trunk, and is led back to his box.

Thousands of pounds' worth of work has been done, yet to an onlooker nothing has happened that resembles mating – no courtship, no effort, no exhaustion. Sloanes admire the understatedness of it all.

But why go to all the trouble to put two animals together, when artificial in-

Covering – like a camel designed by a committee

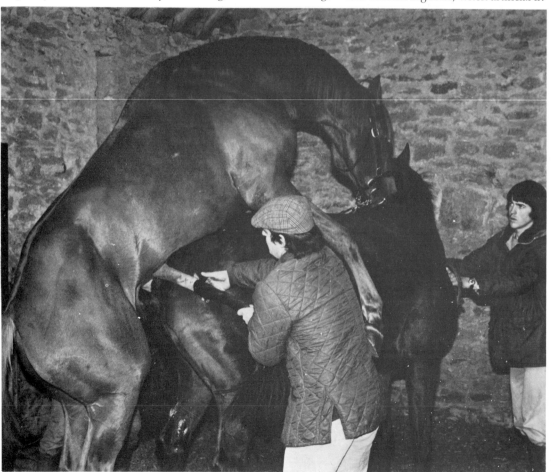

semination could be used with horses as with pedigree cattle? Because the ruling body of breeding in Britain, the Jockey Club, considers, reasonably, that although the use of phials of high-class-stallion semen might be controllable in Britain, Kentucky and Paris, they could get the wrong labels on them in outlying parts of the world.

The wobbly foals are taking their first sunshine on one side of the stable yard as the stallion works to produce next year's crop on the other, in his sacred covering yard.

The garden and larder

Back to work

Snowdrops, crocuses, aconites and primulas are showing brave faces, shaming you as you shiveringly attack the tasks you should have done before. They are:

Servicing the mowers and other machines. Caroline suggests to Henry that they should get a live mower, a Jacob sheep, like the Kimbolton-Smiths. 'Jacob sheep bark apple trees and kill them,' he answers.

Finish the pruning of trees, shrubs and wisteria before the sap starts to rise. You're not alone with your Tarpen or secateurs, you have your Walkman of *Don Giovanni* or Brendel and your remote-control telephone so as not to miss any invitations.

Ordering the seeds. You *may* not get round to it until March if you are having a feeble year.

The struggle with Jack the part-time gardener looms. The only herbs he recognises are mint and parsley, and his main concern is to grow big enough vegetables to win first prize in the local flower show. This cliché is true. Caroline orders the seeds – merely forgetting to include his favourites. But their tug of war continues when he seizes on the free packets enclosed with her order,

Servicing the mower for the war against grass

From Caroline's Diary

Valentine's day. Card from Edward. Sent 7 and none of my children were fooled despite Vanessa's postmark. Better Mum than none. Actually, Sophie got 7, Emma 3, Jamie 4 (3 Fionas) and Edward 1. Nothing from H even though chuckling over young man in his office sending a really filthy one to an articled clerk at Linklaters & Paines where some senior partners' secretaries open everything including Personal. Told him Geoffrey Shakerley always gives Lady Eliz an enamel box from Halcyon Days. 'Second marriage', he said.

THE PISCES SLOANE

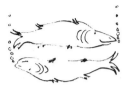

February 19th, enter the Pisces Sloane

You are one Sloane who actually cares about Truth and Beauty. You're not arty-farty, but you *do* know what woods and ornament belong in the eighteenth century, which in the nineteenth. You go to the V & A for more than the postcards. You were born a hundred years too late.

The old-fashioned values and virtues mean a lot to you too. Pride, loyalty, decency, clean underwear – they are what made England great, and what keep you going now. And the children can jolly well go along with them too. Modern life's so *sordid* – they need a background of love and firmness to keep them on the rails.

Modern life also accounts for your disappointment in romantic love. But you work hard at your relationships – and good meals, subtle lighting, flowers all play their part.

You'd go to endless trouble for the perfect sofa material. People who work for you have to appreciate this: 'Now move that oak tree four feet to the left, please, Jack' is not something that every gardener could cope with.

Money has never been important to you as such – but you do need a certain amount to get things *right*. Luckily, there is that small trust fund that manages to squeeze out a few greenies when the drawing-room wants repapering or the children get old enough to need a pool.

Your secret: You may be as sensitive as an acacia, but the old heartwood is pretty strong. You're a survivor.

From Caroline's Diary

Cold, low and in a fearful twit about the children's exams, much more so than they are. Tables and spelling in the car. Trying to lead calm life so they can concentrate.

---

invariably of unSloane flowers, and dots dahlias all through her colour scheme, weeding out her struggling treasures in the process.

By half-term you should have sown garlic cloves in the rose beds to deter the slugs; shallots and rhubarb on the compost heap for the rhubarb crumble and spring-cleaning one's insides. Mummie says that hanging mothballs in the peach tree will prevent leaf curl.

You launch Operation Conservatory. It's traditional to have structural alterations done when the weather is worst. When the builders have made a hole in your outside wall, the snow knows it's time to arrive. The men don't come back for weeks.

You send for the catalogues of Amdega, Dept HG4, Faverdale, Darlington, Co Durham (0325 68522, London office 688 0629) and the smaller Room Outside, Dept HG7, Goodwood Gardens, Waterbeach, near Chichester, Sussex (0243 776563). You discover it will cost you £3,000 *at least* for what you want. 'The only Henry who can afford a conservatory is Henry Ford' says H. Sloane. But you decide to bite into Uncle George's legacy.

Larder and freezer
Too busy gardening or skiing.

Your dog

No village stud need apply
Sloanes go to Cruft's to fall in love with the dogs and to ponder what breed of toy they should get to replace Granny's Ming or which kennels has the husband for Hannah. If it's not to be pedigree it's Battersea Dogs' Home or the RSPCA – *not* a neighbour's bitch's mistake.

Sloanes like all the sporting breeds – hounds, gun dogs, terriers. They do not like what the Kennel Club classifies as Working Dogs (the Queen is an exception, with her corgis). Caroline thinks

Toys are *sweet* (they make Henry *growl*) – Yorkshire terriers, King Charles spaniels, pekes.

Big dogs like Great Danes or mastiffs are not Sloane – they only live eight years, and Sloanes want their four-legged friends around for fourteen – or for ever, if possible.

Neither of the two breeds currently fashionable in Sloanedom is recognised by the Kennel Club: Jack Russells and lurchers.

A bitch comes into season twice a year, for three weeks. All the village dogs haunt your garden, ugly and determined. Even when she's been mated to a pedigree stud dog (fee £45), the hoi polloi dogs try to get their common, *worthless* representatives into the litter. You've sprayed Hannah's bottom, of course, but bitches *want* to be mated and she may slip out and join her swain in the shrubbery.

Gestation takes 63 days. Yor keep one puppy and sell the other five or so, advertising them at eight weeks old, after their inoculations (can charge more. . .). A pedigree Border terrier puppy, for instance, goes for £75.

Just about pays for the villa.

On Henry's mind

● Visiting corporate subsidiaries abroad – South Africa, Malaysia, Australia, America. Must make sure you clock up the executives's tax-saving 30 'qualifying days of absence' before April.

● Checking the mileage on the company car. For maximum tax efficiency it should be more than 2500 miles but less than 18,000.

● The firm's profits announced (it's a 'December' firm – see December).

● Last drinks and last herpes jokes before Lent. Henry's giving up the latter because he wants to surprise Lloyd's. Final fling: *Mistress to lover, 'Darling, I've got something to confess. My husband isn't going bald.' 'You're so adorable – why should I mind?' 'I misheard about his hairpiece.'*

Forward planning

★ Send for application forms for the Dublin Horse Show in August if you want to see the Aga Khan Cup (Friday): Horse Show Ticket Reservations, Royal Dublin Society, PO Box 121, Ballsbridge, Dublin 4.

★ Order wedding invitations NOW, if you want to be a June bride.

Labradors are slobberadors and ours adores lager

From Caroline's Diary

Ash Wednesday. H nervous and restless. Apparently the bar bills in Parliament almost disappear during Lent. H says we should invite all the heavy drinkers now. I boringly gave up sugar.

To dinner with the head of the group. H said he must drink this once, or seem a prig, and Sir Hugh has a famous cellar. I had to drive home, H saying never mind the law, I must fasten my seat-belt so as to not to fall out of the car if the police shoot me!

MARCH

Days 11 hr 50 min (av), lengthening

- ★ Jennifer's Social Dates for the year published in *Harpers & Queen*
- ★ London Designer Collections, first week
- ★ Grand Military Gold Cup, Sandown, Friday
- ★ Rugger internationals (car-park picnics at Twickers, like Badminton – all Sloanes used to go to the West Bar, but due to more restrictions they now make their own fun when weather permits)
- ★ Cheltenham National Hunt Festival, Tues–Thurs mid-month (Gold Cup Thurs)
- ★ The Budget
- ★ Prince Edward's birthday, 10th (b 1964)

- ★ Antiques fairs: Chelsea (1984, 13–24th); Hopetoun House outside Edinburgh (Sloanes head for mahogany and silver and eighteenth-century classics)
- ★ Hunting ends
- ★ Horse and Hound Ball, Grosvenor House; Highland Ball, Claridge's
- ★ British Summer Time starts (1984, 18th; 1985, 17th). Clocks go FORWARD an hour. Less sleep)
- ★ Spring equinox, 21st (it's true about the equinoctial gales)
- ★ Flat racing opens, at Doncaster. The Lincoln is on the last Saturday
- ★ Head of the River race, Mortlake to Putney, Saturday
- ★ School holidays start around 29th

Sloane on the river

Pull, pull together
From March through the summer
March brings back jolly boating weather, the rowing season. Sloanes consider rowing and punting their own preserve – the ones that went to rowing schools anyway (Eton, Shrewsbury, Westminster, St Paul's, Radley, Winchester, Cheltenham, Tiffin, Emanuel, Pangbourne, St Edward's, Hampton . . .). When they get to university, though, they are surprised to find that *other* people row too. The result: Sloanes tend to drop out. After all, you might find yourself pulling behind a Northern chemist – and early-morning training does conflict with a serious study of parties.

The river year is still an important part of the Sloane year. Important dates are:
Head of the River, March
   Thames: Mortlake to Putney
   (Cold, but young Sloanes go)
   It is usually, depending on the tide, the Saturday before
The Boat Race, Oxford v Cambridge
   Thames: Putney to Mortlake
   (Cold, but everybody goes)

Eights Week, Oxford, May
   Thames: along the bit they call the Isis
   (One long party for young Sloanes)
   The above is usually held the week before
Mays, Cambridge, June
   Cam: Along the Backs
   (Another long glorious party for young Sloanes)
Henley, end June-July
   Thames: Temple Island to near the bridge
   (Has risen above rowing into the social firmament – see p 75)
The racing is weirdly different at each event, in response to how much river the Victorian rowing Sloanes had to play with. The Head of the River is timed. The 400 eights – from British colleges, clubs and schools, and European clubs (mostly Dutch and German) – set off seconds apart, so there is always *someone* crossing the line at Putney. One happy year, ferocious waves sunk most of the boats. The German crew began to swim away from theirs, to the delight of the chauvinist Sloane on the PA, who boomed out: 'Will the German crew please return to their boat in accordance with the rules . . . May we remind them

Oxford crew at the Head of the River race after a sinking (the Germans had the last laugh)

The Radley College eight all pee, pee together over the side before a race. But he pees most dangerously who pees alone. If an oarsman finds he can't wait, the boat tends to suddenly rock violently (surprise, surprise) when he is standing and he finds himself arching into the water to join his contribution. Moral: Perfidy begins with a capital Pee.

Caroline to Zara Kimbolton-Smith

Forest Mere, Liphook
Monday

A marvellous idea of Elizabeth's that we spend a week here to do the wedding/dance invites. No wonder Betty comes twice a year. It's quite social – 2 old peers, 3 women with some sort of titles and a pop star. But talk about second schoolhood! Hiding from bores in the shrubbery, getting to know girls from other houses, moaning about teachers, smuggling grub. RRs and other cars worth £0000000s in the drive – lots of noovos, bridge players. Quite a few people on their own, some definitely on the look-out. No dreary health-food types. Ta-ta, must whizz to hydrotherapy pool!

xxx Caro

that deserting a sinking ship is not usual in this country . . . .'

The two-boat Boat Race is pretty boring, since there is little chance of a sinking (though Cambridge did in 1978) and Oxford *always* wins these days (by unfair tactics, Cambridge consider – 'All those American post-grad heavies'). Sophie uses the Boat Race to study the Blues carefully on television so that she knows the stars at Eights and Mays.

The Eights and Mays are bumps races – trying to ram the boat in front – the most exciting kind to row in or watch.

The picnic season

**When gorse is not in flower, then kissing's out of fashion
– country saying**
365 days a year

Forget mess nights and City dinners: the most Sloane celebration is the picnic.

It combines everything: hours of work for Caroline, hours of drinking for Henry, dozens of chances for the dogs to steal food, and a display of ruling-class-ness as you sit at your picnic table (Ascot, Henley) or on your rug (4th of June, Glyndebourne) or stand round your boot (point-to-points) being seen, welcoming friends and impressing enemies from under your hat-brim.

The family is up to God knows what, in different parts of the field, yet everyone, even Caroline, is serene. What is the secret? You are plugged into the *rug*. Sloane families all have two large tartan car rugs from the Scotch House, which would be very expensive to replace, as Mummie keeps telling you. On this rug, the baby learned to crawl, you were sitting when Jamie came out to bat, you first made love, you discovered Dick Francis, you almost committed adultery, Henry got an earwig in his ear ('He's so *obvious*'). The tweedy smell transports you instantly,

Proustianly. The picnic rug is the Sloane Womb.

The food eaten on the rug is a throwback too. In deference to Henry, Caroline rejects her Cordon Bleu training and the Italian pasta they live on now (cheap) and reverts to nursery stodge. Lady Arabella Boxer once described how she unpacked a wonderful haute cuisine picnic alongside a Sloane family's picnic and got shocked looks. Well, exactly. The correct picnic food is *British Edwardian*, with lots of thermoses to add that thermos taste. No taramasalata, pitta bread or other Greekery. No wieners, pastrami or other Americana. Nothing French, not even mustard. Nothing Italian. (But Dutch, Australian or New Zealand products, bottles and *amusing tubes* are fine.)

A Winter picnic
(for 8 eaters, 2 dogs, 20 passers-by, 10 dogs)
Hot soup in thermos, hot sausages in thermos, semi-hot chicken in tin-foil, stodgy cake such as Dundee, Kendal, parkin, Cottenham point-to-point cake.

* *Boot bar*
1 bottle whisky (hidden), 1 hip flask cherry brandy, 1 bottle cherry brandy, 1 hip flask cherry brandy-and-whisky (chisky), 1 bottle sloe gin (just push sloes into the gin bottle and wait), 12 tins beer, 6 bottles (or boxes) Rioja or Muscadet (wine boxes *sound* oikish, but Sloanes love them).
No rum, port or sherry – poncy.

B Spring picnic
Hot sausages in thermos, quiches, pâté, hard-boiled eggs, chocolate cake, coffee.
* Boot bar same.

C Summer picnic, rug
Quiches, cold chicken, cold sausages, crab sandwiches, fruit.
* Add g & t or Pimm's to the boot bar and subtract in proportion.

D Summer picnic, table (sometimes rug)
De luxe picnic. Table has to have chairs separate – not that non-U contraption where it's all-in-one. Table-cloth, linen napkins. Little melons or hot or cold consommé with sherry, smoked salmon and brown bread, cold salmon or chicken in cold savoury sauce, strawberries or raspberries, cream.

From an Army Henry's letter

S·T·A·F·F C·O·L·L·E·G·E S·A·N·D·H·U·R·S·T

Had to act Nanny to a French Major at our dinner night. Everyone there from GOC downwards, everyone dressed to the nines and trying to be typically British to foreign visitors. Halfway through dinner, my Froggy looked a bit fidgety and refused any more wine. At last he asked me 'Where are ze lavatories, if you plees?' I, of course, explained to him that one can't go to the loo in the middle of a mess dinner, but he didn't seem to understand the form. I pointed under the table and said 'Sur le tapis!' but he wouldn't believe it. Then he began to get up. Panic! Froggy was going to disgrace Nanny. Quick as a flash, I demonstrated. He rolled les yeux sauvagement but followed my lead. We both roared with laughter and I told him that the 14th/20th have les pots de chambre d'argent, beaucoup plus civilisé.

* Champagne or Pimm's.
The pop of champagne corks in car-parks is the best sound of summer.

Clever Sloane caterers have moved in on the de luxe picnic, and Sloanes do *love* to be seen unpacking smart boxes saying Fortnum's rather than Caroline's lumpy packets and plastic boxes.

Prepared picnics
(Sometimes Caroline needs a break)
BELGRAVIA CUISINE, 19 Wilton Street, SW1 (352 8805). Hampers for summer events, inc polo.
CLARE'S KITCHEN, Calamansack House, 3 Julia Street, NW5 (485 9441).
DUFF & TROTTER, 71 Palfrey Place, SW8 (582 8373). Gastronomic picnics specially for Glyndebourne, Ascot or the races.
GASTRONOMIQUE, 25 Red Lion Street, WC1 (242 9997).
GILBEY WINE & FOOD COMPANY, 51 Hollywood Road, SW10 (351 1053). Run by OE Sloanes.
GOURMET KITCHEN, 54 Chiltern Street, W1 (935 9756).
NADDER CATERING, Manor Farm House, Dinton, Salisbury, Wilts (Teffont 495).
NUTTALL HAMPERS, The Manor House, Park Road, Stoke Poges, Bucks (Stoke Poges 5323). Pick-up points at Ascot, Wimbledon, the Derby, Henley and Glyndebourne.
PARTY PICNICS, Barrowmead, Shortgate Lane, Laughton, Sussex (Ripe 203). Delivers to Glyndebourne.
RUDD'S, 17 Kensington Court Place, W8 (937 0630) is a Sloane butcher/fishmonger/delicatessen.

Picnic B and the boot bar. 'Forget the horse-box – where's the wine box?'

Picnic D at Henley. The whole dining-room came out of the car-boot

——HAM MOUSSE——

It is not a proper dinner party without the Official Mousse. Sloanes like them for several reasons: they are thought to be slimming, a preoccupation at this time of year; they can be made of pretty well anything (eggs, cheese, chicken, salmon, avocados, raspberries, chocolate...); and by pretty well anyone, in advance. They also have that comfortable, pappy, nursery texture, reminiscent of the beloved chocolate bunny blancmange that Mummie used to make. This mousse can be turned into almost any of the above, by altering the salient ingredients.

For 6

3 tbsp chopped shallot or spring onion ● ½ oz butter ● ¾ pint stock (ham or chicken) ● ½ oz gelatine, softened in 2½ fl oz water or white wine ● 1¼ lb cooked ham ● 2 tbsp sherry ● Salt, pepper, nutmeg ● ¼ pint double cream ● 3 tbsp very finely chopped parsley ● bunch of watercress ● 1 hard-boiled egg

Soften the shallot or onion in the butter in a saucepan for 2-3 minutes, but don't let them colour. Add the stock and heat it to lukewarm. Add the gelatine, which should first be made liquid by standing it, with its water or wine in a cup, in a small pan of simmering water. Cut the ham into small pieces and add them to the stock, onion and gelatine mixture. Whizz this mixture, a little at a time, to a smooth purée in a food processor or liquidiser. Taste for seasoning, add sherry and nutmeg. Chill it in the fridge, stirring occasionally until it is almost set.

Whip the cream until it thickens, but don't let it become too firm. Fold it and the chopped parsley into the ham mixture. Turn it into an oiled 2½-pint-capacity mould. Cover with foil or Clingfilm and leave it to set in a cold place for several hours.

Turn it out on to a dish lined with nice sprigs of watercress and decorate the top with segments or slices of hard-boiled egg.

The garden and larder

Madly busy

Sloane gardens curve with coasts of golden daffodils and forsythia. You take armfuls of daffs to friends in London or the north. Caroline finishes pruning the roses: must be done by end of the month. She may have as many as 200 and it takes 20 minutes a bush, which makes 66 Sloane-hours ... But the birds are singing like lunatics as they build their nests.

Henry reseeds the bald patches on the croquet lawn and puts out saucers of beer for the slugs to fall in and drown. Weeds are peeping cheekily through the cracks in the tennis court.

Caroline manures the asparagus bed and Labby has a major role in it. Jack sows the first lettuces, carrots, onions and 'gharsley parsley' (what Sloanes call it to excuse putting it in and on everything).

Plant herbs throughout the general border and when your open day arrives, rush from one end of the garden to the other pointing out nine different sorts of sage, etc.

On walks, you collect catkins and they drop pollen on the dark lakes of your furniture.

End March or beginning of April, you sow potatoes. Good Friday is the traditional potato date.

Work begins on the conservatory.

Larder and freezer

You're invaded by schoolchildren and Hoorays demanding endless picnics for point-to-points and racing. It's the horse-throat syndrome. If you want to see them you'll have to join them. Caroline *slaves* making shepherd's pies, fish pies, quiches, stews, pâtés, terrines, sausages, sausage rolls, meat loaves, apple pies, apple crumbles, apple Charlottes, plum tarts and plum cakes. She threatens to padlock the freezer.

March

Snow report

Some mud near the bottom of the tows

Heigh-ho for March, the most popular time for unattached Sloanes and young marrieds to go skiing. Many packages now come self-catering – a euphemism for self-eating-out-in-restaurants-every-night. The other type that arrives in March is the hunting Sloane. A pack of them hits the Alps already super-fit and browned by hours in the freezing wind. A hunting Sloane is an early wrinklie.

March is also the time for chalet girls' picnics (spelt pique-nique) – bottles of plonk, huge doorstep sandwiches and a rendezvous at a shepherd's hut. Selected punters are also invited. These revels sometimes are combined with a fancy dress party, and a clutch of polluted clowns (in boiler suits and bright lipstick) somersault down the slopes to a pick-me-up of glühwein or jägertee (rum and tea – lethal!).

Most popular resorts and nightlife places are:

Courchevel. The Supertravel-owned bar Le Jump and Le Tremplin for cocktails.

La Plagne. La Pescalune (*full* of chalet girls).

Méribel. Le Refuge, Le Capricorn and chalet drinks parties – there are at least two of them a night in high season.

St Anton. The Bahnhof bar and the Krazy Kangaroo (the KK).

Tignes. Harry's Bar in Lavachet and Club 2100.

Val d'Isère. The legendary Dick's T-Bar (now a cocktail bar as well), Jacques' Bar. For tea, Les Petites Anglaises, run by two lapsed Sloanes, Amanda Shakespeare and Belinda Boston, who went out on a skiing holiday and stayed.

Verbier. La Luge or the increasingly expensive Farm Club for dancing.

Zermatt. Le Village, dancing in furry moon boots and stone-washed denim jeans.

From Caroline's Diary

Took Hannah to be married, but she hated the grizzled old champion and stuck her bottom in the ground and snarled. Eventually they produced champion's handsome young grandson, whereupon her ears pricked up and she gambolled off with him without a second's hesitation. A real love match, and stud fee for him £15 less!

Re wedding. H says I wouldn't allow the Mannikin Pis to run his own piss-up in a brewery. Annabel is resisting choosing a dress before she's dieted down to photograph weight. However, the BMs' dresses are under way and Eliz announces she will wear RED in some form – Simon's mother said she must decide, so she can. We have got the magazine of the London Designer Collections (£2, from the office, 36 Beauchamp Place, SW3), to see what the new lines are.

The male v. female Shrieking Soprano battle continues. Simon and John think solos are too embarrassing but Annabel wants a Kiri Te Kanawa-type anthem by a friend of a friend who's in the Bach choir. She wanted to come down the aisle to Widor's Toccata but we decided the organist was too fumble-fingered and might reduce the congregation to giggles like the one at Alice's who tried it and got tangled up. She settled for Purcell.

Cheltenham

Jumping for joy

Tuesday to Thursday, mid-March

Last fling of the Sticks Sloanes, who gather unrepentantly, midweek, with their leaders: the Queen Mother, knowledgeable in powder blue and feathers; Prince Charles; Lord Hartington. This is the National Hunt Festival, the jumping championships: sixteen races of which thirteen are professional and three for amateur riders only.

Many Sloanes take a house (the tourist centre in Cheltenham has a list of all accommodation: 0242 22878). If you are invited to a house-party, don't forget hot water bottles (plural), alcohol (plural), evening dress, Alka-Seltzer. It's one long piss-up, and there's no shame in falling asleep at the dinner table.

Punters' pointers

Two unscheduled trains from Paddington connect with buses and deliver you at the entrance (£10 return), and keen punters may collect a tip or two from unwary fellow travellers of the bookmaking 'fraternity' – as Sloanes say – meaning 'Not *our* brothers'. A fraternity of Sloanes is a 'mob'.

The racecourse swarms with Irish priests who clog the bars and betting windows and make signs of the cross over their fancies (Cheltenham coincides with the St Patrick's Day holiday). Best tent is the Turf Club's but (because?) it is a bastion of upper-class male supremacy. Caroline knows that in London a member was sneaked on by a fellow member for helping himself to too much bread-and-butter pudding. Caroline and Henry hope to see a friend who belongs.

They are all ready, in best kit C. As the Anglo-Irish mob wears such marvellous tweeds, great care was taken by both in choosing which suit so as not to look dowdy. They have Cheltenham mem-

TAPES *from* ABROAD

Sloanes love all new devices for communicating – video, Sony Walkman, cordless telephone, tapes. They have taken to sending tapes instead of letters. The whole family chips in. Sophie's cousin Charlotte gets reels of them sent to her in Hong Kong, all of which she wipes clean and reissues with her own round vowels. As she runs your 'letter' through the machine, she interpolates her own comments – she always knows what you are going to say. You do the same to her.

Tape to Hong Kong

'Anyway, darling, your father and I are going to the Pringle-Stuarts for drinks tomorrow...'
('How dreadfully bo-o-oring,' exclaims Charlotte.)
'...Dreadfully boring, darling, I know,' carries on Mummie, 'Daddy wants to talk to you. He thinks he knows what those birds you keep seeing are...'
'Hello, Lottie! Now, do they circle round and round?'
('Yes, yes, they do!' butts in Charlotte.)
'Hmm – thought so,' continues Daddy, 'in that case they *are* eagles...'

Tape from Hong Kong

'I'm going to the Swire's cottage on Lantau this weekend. It's two hours by boat...'
('That's nice – a party of you??')
'Yes a *party* of us, Mummie. Jenny as well. John Coleridge asked me...'
(Daddy: 'I thought the Coleridges had been banned from Hong Kong')...

The Queen Mother knows the form at Cheltenham

March

bers' badges, bought for the day at the gate (£16, £16, £20) or booked beforehand (£45 for the meeting, in 1983, but this closes Friday the week before). (Write to the Steeplechase Co, Cheltenham Racecourse, Prestbury Park, Cheltenham, Glos; 0242 23102.) It's risky to book too far ahead because the weather might force a cancellation.

There are 73 sponsor tents (£1,000 for the meeting, but all taken by November). One of the firms might feed you if you have some connection, and let you watch on their closed-circuit colour telly. Or book in the members' restaurant at least a week before. If no luck, bring your own bulging car-boot.

Everyone carries field-glasses with all their old racecourse badges dangling. One snob remarked 'I don't know why people have so many badges. One gets you in anywhere.' (His said 'Jockey Club'.) Young Sloanes have been known to tie on the cord without the badge: 'Must have drawped off.' Smartest badge for a woman is an enamel gee-gee with your racing colours picked out (Garrard's), worn on the lapel.

Many horsewomen have a complexion like salami. Riding horses is no excuse for *looking* like them. But Michael Dickinson became Caroline's hero by training the first five in the Gold Cup. 'He can salami any time.'

HENRY STUDIES FORM

Henry's arithmetic is not much better than Caroline's and he'll never make a financier, but Form is one area where he does his homework. Caroline deplores all overspending but not £50 to buy both *The Raceform Up-to-date Form Book* and Timeform's *Racehorses of 1983* when they come out in March, plus *Horse and Hound's* annual *Hunter Chasers and Point-to-Pointers* (from the horse bookshop, J. A. Allen's at 1 Lower Grosvenor Place, behind Buck Pal). But she knows Henry gets a lot of fun out of his betting, though she is not convinced by his sums showing he has ended the year 'up'. (If Henry is *really* successful, he won't even cringe at buying the weekly *Timeform Black Book* – £10 every week on the course or £250 for the season; £163 for chasing. From Timeform, Halifax, Yorkshire.)

From Caroline's Diary

Spring-cleaning in the stables. Mr Smith can only fit me in at 8 he's so busy fitting racing plates, shoeing polo ponies etc. A struggle. Glad the RSPCA wasn't around.

Attacked the ponies with the electric clippers, disentangled Pony Club ties from the hay-net, washed the New Zealand rugs in the washing machine. Bad idea. H says his vest and Y-fronts have 3-inch hairs permanently embedded and he now understands why a hair-shirt made you a saint.

THE ARIES SLOANE

March 21st, enter the Aries Sloane

At least you're not dull. Other Sloanes are always saying you're the life of the party. But it's strange how everyone seems to flake out just as you're getting into your stride. You *love* being surrounded by friends – as long as you're boss; 'someone's got to be in charge.' Other people *are* so stolid and over-sensitive. You spend *hours* apologising for what was perfectly reasonable behaviour. (One Arian tipped mint sauce over her husband's head at a DP when he ignored her.) Despite that, you're not usually struck off the list for stand-up-and-shouts.

It doesn't seem to affect the old SA either. Sloane Aries *are* Rangers – a bit naughty with the love 'em and leave 'em routine.

You could do with a bit more of the readies – Sloanes may not like to talk about money, but they can think of plenty of nice things to do with it. As for the house – female Arian Sloanes have better things to do. They were made for living-in staff. The house gets into such a state that after a while even the dogs start giving you looks.

All this rushing about, organising, partying can lead to accidents – tripping over the doormat, Labby; lacquering your hair with deodorant instead of hairspray; putting thank-you notes into the wrong envelopes.

Your secret: You're TERRIFIED of being alone.

---

from Caroline's Diary

H twitching his fingers round apples, hitting sixes with umbrella. Finally he linseeded bat and bought new boots. Now he's ready for flannelled fooling.

On Henry's mind

• Busy money month. Check share transactions for the financial year. If showing a profit of more than the tax-free £5,300, sell loss-making shares to come back inside the total (this is called 'bed and breakfasting'). Sophisticated Sloanes also use the process just to notch each year's capital gain tax-free. Say V. G. Wise-Childe put £10,000 into Sloane Investments at the beginning of a year, and at the end of that year it was worth £15,000, and at the end of the next year it would be £20,000. Selling at the end of year 2 would make him liable for capital gains tax of £1,140. But a 'bed and breakfast' at the end of year 1 would save the pain.

• Edward's 13th birthday on the 12th. Henry girds the paternal loins to have a man-to-man with him (Edward has known for *years*, of course). Very shy Sloane fathers – and widowed mothers – sometimes book the sympathetic family GP.

• Check that the rich who are near and dear to you have given you the maximum under capital transfer tax exemptions – £3,000. Tax-saving is, after all, the one socially acceptable reason for asking for money for oneself.

• Stock up on wine before the Budget.

• Job-hunting season for Sloanes in their last year at university. The University Appointments Committee gets active after Christmas and the young male Sloane sees the big British corporations before Easter.

• Talking of careers, Henry has another Stock Exchange joke: *A doctor, an architect and a Lloyd's broker are discussing which has the cleverest dog. The doctor calls to his dog, Bones. 'Do it, boy' says the doctor. The dog runs off, digs up bones and builds a skeleton. The architect calls to his, Set Square. The dog rushes about, collects branches and builds a kennel. The broker says 'That's really awfully good. Come on, Bullshit!' His dog screws the other two, takes a three-hour lunch break and pisses off home early.*

Forward planning

★ Send off for brochure and booking form for Glyndebourne tickets (p 61).

★ Book for Goodwood car-park and Members' dining-room (p 83).

★ Write to St James's Palace for voucher for Royal Ascot (p 70).

★ Buy tickets for the summer music festivals – Aldeburgh, Stour, Bath etc.

★ Buy tickets and book your eligibles for the Season's balls.

APRIL

Days 13 hr 52½ min (av), lengthening

★ April Fool's Day, 1st (Sloane telephones friends in an assumed voice offering super paid-in-cash evening job: please let him know at this number – the VD clinic)

★ Trout fishing starts on most trout rivers, 1st

★ Start of the financial year, 6th

★ The Boat Race, Oxford v Cambridge, Putney to Mortlake, first Saturday (or late March)

★ Cricket season opens (Sloanes love Lord's)

★ Polo season opens (more cocaine than Sloane)

★ Driving season opens (not very Sloane but Prince Philip leads the way)

★ Grand National at Aintree

★ Black and White Ball, Café Royal (debs coming up to the starting line)

★ Berkeley Dress Show, Berkeley Hotel (start of the debs' race)

★ Badminton horse trials, Thursday to Sunday mid-month

★ Maundy Thursday (1984, 19th; 1985, 4th). Names of new QCs in *The Times* and *Daily Telegraph* (barrister Henrys have been betting on who's getting it)

★ Good Friday (1984, 20th; 1985, 5th) (most stately homes open their season so Sloane guides are on. Plant the potatoes)

★ Easter Sunday (1984, 22nd; 1985, 7th) (go to church – Vicar's pay day)

★ Easter Monday (1984, 23rd; 1985, 8th): point-to-points

★ Queen's real birthday, 21st (b 1926)

★ Whitbread Gold Cup, Sandown, Saturday (end of the jumping season, Sloanes consider)

★ Back to school around 24th: exam term

★ Back to university: exam term

★ Newmarket, last Thurs to Sat (or first in May). 1,000 Guineas Thursday, 2,000 Guineas Saturday (thronged with Cambridge undergraduates – last big outing before exams)

The Grand National

I was GLUED to Becher's

Saturday end March or beginning of April
You must go at least once. It's not the same on the box.

Sloanes love the special Sloane train (it chugs in your heart with the Orient Express and the Royal Highlander). This train, all reserved, 200 seats, leaves Euston at 8.26, *after* the special diesel train for hoi polloi (8.10), but gets there first. It whizzes you electrically to Liverpool in your Pullman while you eat your four-course-breakfast, then buses take you to the course at Aintree. Your train is £40 return with two meals, theirs is £20 without meals (but dining-car). You reserved in February, but there are always parties cancelling so don't despair (01-387 9400).

All the Sloanes are in kit B, but men in worsted rather than tweed: it's a *town* race. If you don't end the day in the train you'll end it at the bar of the Adelphi hotel in Liverpool. You can get a members' enclosure badge at the gate if not sold out (£25), but it's wiser to write for it first (Aintree Racecourse, Liverpool; 051 523 6520; £35 for three-day meeting, in 1983).

Delicious lunch in the members', unreserved (rush in and book when you arrive) or reserved (booking from Christmas). Lots of £50 bets being laid. It's such a long race, four-and-a-half miles, with 30 huge jumps, that three-quarters of the entries just won't get round. Which leaves a possible three or four to choose from. Henry says he *always* gets the winner of the National. You need a big horse, a stayer, and in wet weather a slogger; mighty, super-human.

It's so emotional, Caroline gets pissed and giggly over dinner on the train. Silly unhorsy Sloanes sometimes get married on Grand National Saturday, when everybody but them is *glued* to telly. Then it's a case of lugging the portable along. The church is empty while the

Modelling the Boat Race style

guests sit in their cars and watch it to the end, then sprint breathlessly in a mob into the aisle.

Snow report

Fresh Sloanefalls on the piste

The last Saturday in March is *the* day for young Sloanes to set off skiing: the beginning of the Easter holidays.

Val d'Isère is the favourite, but all Sloane resorts are snowed under with Rangerettes, aged 15 or 16, with their families or, better still, other people's families. A few come unsupervised. Both sexes wear Puffas and a headband of folded scarf or shoelace. Romances started on the slopes can launch a term's letters.

This holiday marks Sophie's and Jamie's initiation into drunken debauchery. One gang included royal Rangerette Lady Helen Windsor, but the French can't read the woolly-scarf-and-Barbour uniform and think they are young British yobs.

In 1983, the new mayor actually issued a warning to Hooray Heavies – behave or else he'd *halve* the number of beds available to Brits. Does he honestly think they'd notice? But enough of the sales cochons, the espèces d'ordure. . . .

Recently, April has been a problem month for chalet girls. Strict authorities who grant them their three-month work permits have started to deport girls who overstay their welcome.

The Flat

The sport of king-size-Bentleys (but Sloanes get a look-in)

End March to mid-November

THEY'RE OFF! shout the newspapers every year about the Doncaster meeting,

Boat Race '83, the Oxford crew muscle- and Mortlake-bound

the first flat racing of the season. They're all off, the unknown quantities – the two-year-olds – and the really interesting horses – the three-year-olds, embarking on a year that might include the Derby or the Arc.

The two-year-olds have their own important races: the Dewhurst, the Cheveley Park Stakes, the Middle Park, the Futurity. But the best three-year-olds are entered for the Classics. There are five Classics, but in practice it is possible to win only three of them (the Triple Crown).

2,000 Guineas, 1 mile, colts and fillies, Newmarket, early May.

1,000 Guineas, fillies, same course, two days later of same meeting.

These rather short distances are a test of speed on a straight course.

Derby, 1½ miles, mostly colts (fillies may enter), Epsom, June.

A great test for a horse, who has to be able to gallop uphill and downhill and negotiate Tattenham Corner (several short-priced favourites have failed the latter and ended up almost in the cheap stands).

Oaks, fillies, same course, three days later of same meeting.

St Leger, 1¾ miles, both sexes, Doncaster, September.

Requires relentless galloping ability, staying-power and acceleration at the end.

But if you only race in your backyard, all you get is a backyard reputation. Owners want the final test against older horses and younger nations, which is:

Arc de Triomphe, 1½ miles, both sexes, all ages from three, Longchamp, October (200 metres = 1 furlong: the only friendly metric conversion). This is where the ages and nations' stock are compared. There has hardly ever been a bad Arc winner but there have been many poor Derby winners.

These are the peaks of Henry's racing year. However, viewed socially (ie by Caroline), there are four Flat meetings she knows she must attend:

Royal Ascot, June.

Show class – dress up, but not like the noovos.

Goodwood, end July.

Stamina – windproof clothes, anchored hat.

Ayr, September. 'The Western Meeting' as it is known to People. Tweeds, very good brooch on velvet beret.

The Arc (as Ayr).

Go with fellow Sloanes, or the Froggies will make you feel uncouth.

The Champion Stakes, 1¼ miles, run at Newmarket in mid-October, is another big all-aged race. Attendance by Henry and Caroline, however, is optional.

Betting Henry and Beginner's Luck Caroline

Henry finds the flat much more difficult than jump races. Henry, asked at a dinner for his favourite quotation, said

Dear Granny

Thank you very much for my cigarette cards (?)
Bit funny-looking though – I've put them in my collection. It's quite strange how they're all green with a picture of the Queen on one side. Odd!

I hope you're getting the same weather as us – ie a howling gale and a constant April shower. Grate fun! Of course, when it isn't raining, I hope you're outside jogging, training hard for next year's Marathon. No seriously, I think you ought to enter. It would be good fun.

Well seeing as how I've just mentally exhausted you and myself I'd better go.

Love from
Harold Azlett

Edward's thank-you letter to Granny (aged 80) after his 13th birthday

'Eleven to two Baulking Green' (the great hunter-chaser and punter's friend).

When betting, Henry considers five factors:

1 *Recent form.* How has it been doing against the opposition?

2 *Handicap.* Is it carrying too much weight to win? If a horse did well last time he raced he might be obliged to carry up to a stone more than an equally good horse who unaccountably (ha ha) ran very slowly.

3 *The going.* A last-minute factor. Horses often have a flat action or a rounded, pounding action (stayers and jumpers). Obviously, a flat-actioned horse can't skate – fly – in mud, so he needs 'firm' or 'good' going. But after rain, the pounder comes into his own, ploughing on like the tortoise when his hare-like opponent, who can't pick his feet up, is anchored and demoralised.

The papers give the going in the morning on a scale of six: 'hard', 'firm',

'good', ('dead' – usually omitted) 'good to soft', 'soft' or 'heavy'. When Henry says a dinner party bore is heavy going, he knows what it means.

4 *Horses for courses.* Does the distance suit? Some horses show a marked preference for certain courses – just like Sloanes and for much the same reasons.

5 *Paddock performance.* Is the horse sweating? ('leaving the race behind in the paddock'). Tail swishing? (hates the world). Unfit? (girth biting into a roll of fat). Throwing head? (doesn't want to race). Ears pricked? (wants to race).

Henry bets regularly and often wins, though not over the long haul. His bookie is Heathorn's. (The other smart persons' bookie, the late Archie Scott, was ruined by a £5 bet by the Dowager Duchess of Norfolk. It was an accumulator and all six horses came in, leaving him owing her £35,000. He clapped both hands to his hat and cried 'Desperation, desperation' and he had to sell out, to William Hill.)

Betting Caroline considers three factors:

1 *Name.* O'Henry, Friday Cottage, Private Label, Princes Gate, Our Dynasty – you like anything that relates to the life of Mrs Sloane. Sometimes these mad choices actually win, to Henry's chagrin.

2 *Owner/trainer/rider.* The Queen's and Queen Mother's horses always carry a ton of female Sloane 50p bets. Sloane women don't *actually* bet on pretty silks – that's a vile slander. But they like to show that they recognise some, eg Lord Derby's black top, white cap or Lord Rosebery's rose and primrose.

They go for jockeys they know, like Lester Piggott. He's a sallow, unsmiling person but with Sloanes auld acquaintance is three-quarters of the battle.

They go for trainers they like. A surprising number of trainers are Sloane. Caroline follows Guy Harwood (non-Sloane), Henry Cecil, John Dunlop (Flat); and Michael Dickinson, Fred Win-

It is impossible to pick a winner without a perfectly-cut tweed jacket

ter (non-Sloane), Mrs Mercy Rimell (National Hunt).

3 *'My own theory'*. Something like 'the first horse out of the paddock to go up to the start' sounds silly, but Caroline won several races on it.

Caroline bets with the Tote. She usually makes a little money, because 'I might as well stop now I'm ahead.' She doesn't see why Henry feels he must support the industry by contributing £5 to every race. She registers her displeasure by refusing to lend him money for a drink afterwards.

The debutante season

Your U lamb

April to July

In England, the girls risk the bright months. In the rest of Europe – including Scotland – they come out in the dark, like glow-worms. But whatever the weather, many Sloanes still feel they must launch a daughter. Cecils and Sackville-Wests do not come out – why should they? But Sloanes, like the noovos they decry, must put hostesses under *some* obligation to invite Sophie, to widen her net for the Hon Rupert Right. Some parents hope she'll find him at university – but what if she only has enough O-levels for the University of Life? She can't just be left to Gary Wrong of Sales.

Parents whose ewe lamb (Sloane for daughter) 'isn't actually coming out, we're just giving a drinks party/barbecue and records in the garden' hope she will be asked to a few big balls given by schoolfriends or country neighbours.

The idea of a formal début is fashionable again – a summer flower-bed of innocent, eligible (rich) girls in white: though anybody can see they have three holes in one ear and one in the other and have been on the pill since they were fifteen. The official coming-out ball has started again in Paris, which had given it

> ### From Caroline's Diary
>
> *How I hate the Pony Club. Ponies just over laminitis from gorging on grass, and they and I driven potty by Emma's determination to win the Prince Philip cup. Every third day putting up poles, packing lunch box, unpacking horse-box, stiffening the querulous upper lip. Bankrupting ourselves paying for crisps and more sodium glutamate soup and entry money.*

up, and the deb ball is the high point of the year and symbol of social immobility in Charleston (photographs forbidden), Baltimore, Montreal, etc. Caroline can't quite believe it, 'in this day and age!' She herself belongs to the anti-deb 1940s and '50s generation, like the Queen, who stopped presentation at Court in 1958. But having seen Nadia Noovo beat Sophie to the post throughout the Pony Club years, she decides to Make An Effort.

In November, mothers solicit the help of 'Jennifer', whom *The Debrett Season* calls 'the doyenne of Society': Mrs Betty Kenward of *Harpers & Queen*. She publishes Jennifer's Social Dates for the year in the March *Harpers & Queen*, plus lists of caterers, marquee firms, discos etc. She is 'incredible', formidable in her complete outfits in very bright colours, like the Queen's, with matching velvet bow behind her stiffly-rolled silver hair. She can tell a novice when and where to have the party: say, drinks at the Dorchester.

Debs' parents give approximately 80 drinks parties, 40 dances. About 200 girls are doing the season (but often two mothers share a party). The best dances are in stately homes in the country, when young Blogtonshire meets London's cocaine-sniffers and pushers, to their mutual delight.

Party Planners is the smartest firm by far to organise your party. It is the 23-year-old brainchild of Lady Elizabeth Anson, wife of camera-clicking Sir

Betty Kenward, Queen of the Season

Peter Townend (back, with cig) keeps a list if you haven't enough men. Here he is with bandleader Andrew Chance (left) and Gigi Letts (front) at her dance at Hurlingham

Geoffrey Shakerley, sister of camera-clicking Lord Lichfield, cousin of camera-clickee the Queen.

More congenial to Henry's bank statement is Mrs George Dare, 9 Launceston Place, W8 (937 7072). Mrs Dare organises parties in her 1840 (Listed) house with a studio and paved lit garden.

Ordinary Sloanes should have their party mid-season (say, the second Wednesday in June). Send out invitations six weeks ahead. You will then be asked to everyone else's, but they will not be too blasé to come to yours, as they will be by July. The actual invitations can be quite dashing, possibly even on a balloon.

To get enough of the right people to ask, Caroline has been scurrying around since March, when she took a flat in Ennismore Gardens as a London base. Of course, she has been quietly assembling eligibles of Sophie's age for seventeen years, but now she becomes barefaced. There are three cocktail parties a night in the season, and Sophie must be asked, and the stars must come to Sophie's. Mothers get together in Italian trattorias to form alliances. You make new friends for life, and discover what bitches some of your old friends are. The mothers used to have to do it all, but the daughters are much more involved now ('Ma's hopeless').

You give and go to mother-and-daughter lunch parties and tea parties, in hotels (a bit downmarket), at home or even in a daughter's shared flat. It's an unashamed rat-race – pens out for

From Caroline's Diary

Missing Edward terribly. H has sent him into exile in London with John and Eliz to do holiday crash cricket course at Lord's, rings him every night to quiz him on his nets work. I suddenly realise how much the balance of the hols depends on my calm little fellow. Hysteria is mounting.

---

names, dates, addresses. Mrs Noovo's cock-a-hoopoe as she writes down Lady Snooks's home number (it's in the telephone book; it's Mrs Noovo who is ex-directory).

'The list' (of debs' delights) does exist. It is kept by Peter Townend, social editor of *Tatler* and a former editor of *Burke's Peerage*. He is as unSloane as Mrs Kenward is crisp, and they may not be placed at the same table. He is a great verifyer of facts for newspaper gossip columnists – Mrs Kenward will not speak to them. He lives in a flat in

April

⁂A⁑CAUTIONARY⁑TALE⁑

And absolutely true
One absent-minded heir to a peerage was asked by so many unknown hostesses that he wrote to the next one:

Dear Mrs Murray
*   Thank you for your kind invitation to the dance for your daughter, but I am afraid I do not accept invitations from people I do not know.*

The answer came:

Dear Johnny,
*   I am so sorry you do not remember me. I am your Aunt Mary (your father's first cousin), and we have met frequently at Blogton. The whole family will be so disappointed not to see you.*

Chelsea Towers, Chelsea Manor Street (352 2952), with leather-bound *Tatlers*, *Burke's*, *Debrett's* and dozens of photographs of himself at dances.

Peter Townend knows when all smartie girls are about to be seventeen. He writes to their mothers in November or December, in turquoise ink and flowery handwriting, avoiding the words 'season' and 'debutante' but asking 'Is your daughter likely to be around next year?' He works hard to get 40 or 50 smart debs. The other, less smart 150 contact *him*. But it is essential to have enough smart ones to maintain the tone.

He can give you names and addresses of 60 to 200 young men 'to make up numbers', if he approves of you. Though called debs' delights, they are not amazingly *amusing*. But they are rent-a-tie, will come in dinner-jacket, and your father will prefer them to the ones you prefer.

Some men on Peter Townend's list are recycled until they are 28 or 29. (Haven't earring, will travel.) But despite this dedication to duty, he is not paid by mothers for his valuable social work. You can try to ask him out to lunch but he is always booked seven or eight weeks ahead.

His own drinks party is the unofficial opening of the season. No press allowed. It's a rather awkward occasion, since nobody yet knows each other.

The official occasions one must go to are quite few. Dates of the dances are in *The Times*, *Daily Telegraph*, *Scotsman* and Jennifer's Diary, beginning in February, with where to buy the tickets (at around £20 to £30). (See also p 104).

You *must* make up a party. You will see several square uncles plugging round holes suddenly left by a rent-a-tie.

The official Season
Berkeley Dress Show, Berkeley Hotel, mid-April, for NSPCC. 20 girls model, having been given a week's free training by Lucie Clayton College in deportment, catwalking etc. Mrs Sally Walton, NSPCC (580 8812).
Royal Caledonian Ball, Grosvenor House, mid-May. Scottish, white tie, heartiest solid-gold deb occasion. Some English debs take reel lessons beforehand, and there is a rehearsal at 4 on the day. Princess Margaret always goes, in the Duke of Atholl's party. Mrs Rupert Hazlerigg (622 6074).
Rose Ball, Grosvenor House, mid-May. *The* deb ball – took over from Queen Charlotte's (d 1976) (the Harlots' Hop) where lines of debs curtseyed to a huge cake. 1,200 people, awful dinner, too many raffles and tombolas. Mrs Laurie Weston (748 4824).

If you have done all this, and put in an appearance at Royal Ascot, Henley and Goodwood, at six Young Balls (p 18) and at three dozen private parties, you have done a Season. Your father has spent at least £5,000 on it. He hopes you keep your nice new friends and lose the druggies.

One needs firm control for the pas-de-basque

Caroline to Zara Kimbolton-Smith

Have been slaving away at the debs' mums' teas. Sophie and I have made some pals and I am stalking 2 or 3 promising pairs. I thought someone was stalking us last week! A wire-haired noovo, like someone in Dysentery, was all over me. Wondered why until she said 'You are Lady Jones, aren't you?' 'Sorry, but it is only the humble Mrs Sloane that you see before you.' Instant *departure! (Jamie's not partnering* her *monster.) Oh well.* xxx Caro

The dress for your wedding or coming out

London

Designers
TOM BELL, 65c New King's Road, SW6 (373 1775)
BELLVILLE SASSOON, 73 Pavilion Road, SW1 (235 5901)
CAROLINE CHARLES, 9 Beauchamp Place, SW3 (584 2521)
DAVID AND ELIZABETH EMANUEL, 26a Brook Street, W1 (629 5569)
GINA FRATINI, 2 New Burlington Place, W1 (734 0125)
THEA PORTER, 1a Avery Row, W1 (499 4260)
ZANDRA RHODES, 14a Grafton Street, W1 (499 6695)

Antique dresses
ANTIQUARIUS, 135 King's Road, SW3
   MR GUBBINS at Antiquarius (351 1513)
   SUZANNE LEVERINGTON at Antiquarius (731 0236)
CATHERINE BUCKLEY, 302 Westbourne Grove, W11 (229 8786)
TATTERS, 74 Fulham Road, SW3 (584 1532) (New dresses in old lace etc)

Shops
HARRODS, Knightsbridge, SW1 (730 1234)
HARVEY NICHOLS, Knightsbridge, SW1 (235 5000)
LIBERTY'S, Regent Street, W1 (734 1234)

Private dressmakers
AMANDA BARBER, 3 Albany Mansions, Albert Bridge Road, SW11 (228 7315)
TATTI BOURDILLON, 54 Charleville Road, W14 (381 5592)
VIVIEN FOORD-KELSEY, Peacock's Wood, Little Gaddesden, Herts (044 284 3578)

TOM SZARWESKI, 16 Lower Common South, SW15 (788 9538)

Country and Scotland
ANNABELINDA, 6 Gloucester Street, Oxford (Oxford 246806)
ROBERTA BUCHAN, 104 Morningside Road, Edinburgh (Edinburgh 447 8549) and 176 Hope Street, Glasgow (Glasgow 332 6060)
GRACE ELLIOTT, 35 Friar Street, Worcester (Worcester 20861)
MELITA, Town House, High Street, Chobham, Surrey (Chobham 6308)
ANDREA WILKIN, 159 Adnitt Road, Northampton (Northampton 31384)

The shoes
ANELLO & DAVIDE, 94 Charing Cross Road, WC2 (836 5019) for satin pumps
MANOLO BLAHNIK, 49 Old Church Street, SW3 (352 8622)
CLIVE SHILTON at RAYNE, 57 Brompton Road, SW3 (589 5560) and 15 Old Bond Street, W1 (493 9077)

The wedding reception or coming-out party
In London, any of the great *old* hotels, or Searcy's (a house; such nice proportions), or your club.
THE BERKELEY, Wilton Place, SW1 (235 6000)
CLARIDGE'S, Brook Street, W1 (629 8860)
THE DORCHESTER, Park Lane, W1 (629 8888)
GROSVENOR HOUSE, Park Lane, W1 (499 6363)
HYDE PARK HOTEL, 66 Knightsbridge, SW1 (235 2000)
THE ORANGERY, Holland Park, W11 (c/o Party Planners)
PARK LANE HOTEL, Piccadilly, W1 (499 6321)

THE RITZ, Piccadilly, W1 (493 8181)
THE SAVOY, Strand, WC2 (836 4343)
30 PAVILION ROAD, SW1 (Searcy's) (584 3344)

For the thrash
DISCOS FOR HIRE
Bentley's, 4 Leinster Mews W2 (262 6264). DJs: Peregrine Armstrong-Jones, Nicholas Lumsden.
Bubbles (Salisbury 23386). DJ: Paul Honeywood.
Chatters, 35 Marlborough Court, Walton Street, SW3 (584 2909). DJs: Timothy Radford, Roland Chamberlain, David Beamish.
Gibson's, c/o Party Planners, 56 Ladbroke Grove, W11 (229 9666). DJs: Angus Gibson, James Cronin.
Joffin's, 134 Lots Road, SW10 (351 4333). DJs: Jonathan Seaward and four assistants.
Juliana's, 217 Kensington High Street, W8 (937 1555). DJs: William Bartholemew and six assistants.
Shews, 4 Edith Grove, SW10 (352 5414). DJs: Piers and Barnaby Thompson, James Radice.
Zinos, 217 Kensington High Street, W8 (937 3036). DJs: Richard Leuchars, Charles Mayhew.

BANDS
Chance, 313 Brompton Road, SW3 (584 3206). Led by Andrew Chance.
Dark Blues, c/o Party Planners, 56 Ladbroke Grove, W11 (229 9666).
Jazz with a Tune, 13 Wandsworth Plain, SW18 (874 0131).
New Cavendish Dance Band, 14 Amisfield Place, Longniddry, East Lothian (Longniddry 52207). Specialise in reeling.

April

Badminton and Three-Day Eventing

Hooray for HRH

The Queen always goes to *Badmington* so so do you. She loves Princess Anne and Mark Phillips, you love Lucinda Prior-Palmer Green and Richard Meade. The big events are Badminton, Burghley and Wylye. The views of Badminton House (a palace), Burghley House (a palace), and Bathampton House (a big house, merely) in their beautiful parks are a permanent attraction. The actual testing of the horses in a three-day event takes four days, and is little understood by the dreaded *Sloanes who go for fun*. They only come on Saturday, for the cross-country, when the horses jump a terrifying course of about 30 huge obstacles.

You walk round the course with the other 100,000 spectators (at Bad and Burg): a few individualists go the opposite way. Each dangerous jump has its audience of hopeful grockles drinking beer from plastic cups which they then throw on the ground. But the Sloanes go back to the tent village to watch on closed-circuit colour television. It is shown in the sponsors' tents, the club tents, the big trade tents – you're sure to know *someone* who'll let you watch. Television has been the most wonderful addition to Sloane sporting life – you can actually see what's happening for the first time, instead of not daring to ask the snooty Captains, Majors, Davinas and Plunkets. It's a good idea to join the BHS, so you can use their tent at all horse events. (Joining fee £5.75, subscription £11 over 21, £7 under 21,

Went with Annabel to Tom Bell's for fitting of the wedding dress. Ivory ribbed silk, costs a fortune.

Annabel still neurotic about whether she'll shrink to size 10 or swell to 14! Told her story of fat woman who went on a diet but didn't lose weight. One day friend called and found her eating suet pudding. 'Have you stopped the diet?' 'No, I had the diet two hours ago. This is dinner.' La Belle not v amused. Snapped at the fitter.

A tricky jump at Badminton attracts hopeful crowds: 'Off! Off! Off! Off!'

British Horse Society, Stoneleigh, Kenilworth, Warwickshire; 0203 52241.)

If not eating caterer food in one of these tents, you have brought the Sloane boot picnic. The car-park is Sloane heaven – rows of Volvos, Peugeots, XR3i's, Range Rovers, BMWs, Renault 5s, Golfs, Land-Rovers, with the dogs tied to the back bumper. *Not* table and champagne at Badminton, these are noovo and only seen behind Rollers. The eventing picnic is menu B (p 34), plus the occasional experiment from Winkfield or Prue Leith. Anything a dog can eat.

What's really happening
The horses and riders are tested in dressage, Thursday and Friday, and roads-and-tracks, steeplechase and cross-country on Saturday. On Sunday, when they are tired but still ready to have a bash jumping fast and stretched out (as in the cross-country), they have to come back to up-and-down show-jumping in the ring. This is where the competition is usually lost. But a great rider can get his or her horse back: sometimes it requires riding it at intervals all night to keep it supple.

The caravanserai
Trade stands now accompany all big Sloane outdoor events, and ye little village of Sloane Magna springs up where you can buy all your favourites – from Almost Unwearoutable Socks to

whoopee cushions (from the joke shop patronised by the royal family – the Tetbury Furniture Store).

One up
To know a competitor. You recognise Pony Club acquaintances on the programme – 'Come on, Rachel!' – but real one-upmanship is to see a rider you know walking and be acknowledged by her/him.

One down
To be heard referring to the Duke of Beaufort as 'Master' is as vulgar as the *Sun* calling HRH 'Charlie', unless you were in the Beaufort Pony Club or have hunted with the Beaufort for most of your life.

The correct pronunciation
Sloanes say 'Badmington'. Sloanes spell and talk entirely phonetically (the bookcase at home has a glass front so you can't be expected to open that). They misspell Burghley as Burley or Burleigh. They think it's debencher, Pereguin, batchelor (wish Peregrine Hartington *was* a bachelor).

The big Events
Badminton, April, Avon. Owner: the Duke of Beaufort. Entrance payable at the gate. Horse Trials office: 045 421 272.
Burghley, early September, Stamford, Lincolnshire. Owner: the Marquess of Exeter. Not *quite* as smart socially as Badminton (too far from London; Queen not guaranteed), but very similar. A nicer park, and the trees are out. You can pay to become a Member of Burghley and use their marquee. Horse Trials office: 0780 52131.
Wylye, early October, near Salisbury, Wiltshire. Owner: Lord Hugh Russell. The horse trials have been combined with a driving event since 1982. Wylye is probably the most Sloane event; grockle-free; muddy; a lower-level competition

April

From Caroline's Diary

Easter Sunday. Lunch for the Pyratt-Smiths. The first post-Lent g & t's heaven. They and Pam's personality extremely exhilarating. I do wish she was here all year but we might not be able to stand it. Noble of them to live in greasy Marbella to pay for schooling the rather grumpy silent Rodney. Emma's efforts to get him out of his shell resisted. He

wouldn't find the Bendicks eggs round the garden, painstakingly laid by Jamie and me, so the magpies will find them in the summer and get chocolate beaks.

Took the party to the castle after lunch, to help support Jane on her first day – but no need, pullulating hoi polloi. Magnolias magnificent. Pam accosted the old earl hiding like an ostrich in his battered fishing hat. He looked terrified but she soon had him chatting. Hope he doesn't have a relapse.

Change appt fitting for Ascot clothes.

so you're bound to know someone riding; no obligation to walk the course. Event office: 09856 238.

The Sloane as fisherman

Henry is lured away

Where's the list of opening dates, you might ask. There *is* no list. Even Hardy's, the fisherman's heaven in Pall Mall, has not compiled one. Trout are different from salmon, and different rivers have different dates, and a stretch of the river may be different again. For salmon, there are spring rivers and summer rivers. There are best times on all the rivers. The season mostly ends in September.

Fishing is not central to Sloanedom like riding, since it requires silence and solitude. And ghillies don't chat, they put ye doon. 'Ye should hae been here last week' they say (like gardeners), then they tell you about the American gentleman who said 'A goddam fish has just bitten the bug offa my string' and you imagine what they will say about you and what the American's tip was.

But fishing transcends even the disadvantage of being only a one-person picnic (at best two). It puts you in communion with nature – and Eng. lit. Sloanes consider fishing to have the best writing of all sports, in *The Compleat Angler*, Lord Grey of Falloden's *Fly Fish-*

ing and John Waller Hills's *A Summer on the Test*.

There is a growing form of middle-class fly fishing, in big reservoirs like Rutland Water and Graffham Water, which have been stocked with rainbow trout. Your rainbow might be 19 lb – it may be very v pro, but it's not v U.

Working-man's fishing, 'coarse fishing for the coarse' – bait fishing in local gravel pits etc – is the most popular sport in the country. Thank God. That'll keep the Reds out of the salmon spawning beds (or redds, as they are confusingly called). June 16th is *their* opening day.

But real Sloane fishing is for salmon, sea trout and brown trout, with a fly in rivers. It's full of skill. It's full of frustration. Even if you impersonate an insect perfectly, the trout may not be biting (thanks, fellas – this beat is only costing me £70 a day), and the salmon have absolutely no need to, ever, as they are the great fasters and needn't eat for the six months or more between re-entering their home river and spawning.

It was a bad day for salmon and Sloanes when the desperate Danes discovered where salmon go in their two years at sea – Greenland and the Faeroes. The netters moved in. Net a shoal, kill a river – salmon famine.

British rivers themselves are less hospitable now that the Forestry Commission has planted massed conifers.

...and we can serve the sea-lice separately!

Too-quick drainage send the rivers up and down like a washing machine, not to mention the acid rain caught in the trees and funnelled down. Not to mention the poachers with nets.

Getting out on the beat

First rank: be invited. You love the lodge/ghillies fine malt whisky/big landowner combination. Compliments for fishing is the motto – cadge, wangle, invite them to the opera. Sir Marcus Kimball in Sutherland is very hospitable.

Second rank: you rent a lodge with salmon fishing, eg Balnacoil with the Brora. This costs thousands of pounds and has to be rebooked the minute you finish the current holiday. Outsiders rarely get a bite.

Third rank: you rent fishing and stay at a hotel, like the expensive little inn at Rosehall by Lairg, or the Arundel Arms on the Tamar. Fishing hotels own beats and let them. The estate agents also manage and let fishing rights: Jamie Illingworth of Strutt & Parker; Bell & Ingram or Smith Gore of Carlisle; Knight Frank & Rutley or Savills.

Or you can be in a syndicate and go down for a day a week – £500 to £600 a year for a good bit of the Test or Itchen (trout).

Casting ouch

We've booked at the Aching Arms. It's difficult to cast elegantly – so Sloanes usually don't. Henry loses his fly, or gets it caught in a willow, or in Caroline who is standing behind him. Caroline finds fishing easier with the new carbon fibre rods (Hardy's or Farlow's in Pall Mall). She always manages to land the biggest fish; Henry says it's a compleat fluke.

The Houghton Club (twelve members) based on the Grosvenor Arms at Stockbridge is the most exclusive club in the world. They're all frightfully rich and cast like Croesus.

A GRATIN OF SALMON

Just occasionally, when the fishing goes well, Henry is able to give Caroline more salmon than she knows what to do with. More usually, there's just enough left over from last night's dinner to make lunch for two, but not enough for lunch for six, which is the number she's faced with at Easter. This recipe solves the problem. She saves the liquid the salmon's been poached in, and uses what's left of the white wine, for the sauce. Hard-boiled eggs provide extra bulk. Actually this isn't bad with *tinned* salmon.

For 6

3 large onions, sliced ● 1 oz butter ● 1 tbsp oil ● 4 hard-boiled eggs ● 10 oz cooked salmon ● 1 pint white wine sauce (see below) ● 3–4 tbsp dry breadcrumbs plus a few knobs of butter

Preheat the oven to 375°F (gas 5). Soften the onions in the butter and oil. Slice the hard-boiled eggs. Skin, bone and flake the salmon. Put alternating layers of onion, egg and salmon in a gratin dish and dribble the sauce over it as you go. Finish with a sprinkling of breadcrumbs dotted with butter and bake it in the oven for 30 minutes.

White wine sauce

1½ oz butter ● 1½ oz flour ● ½ pint fish stock ● ¼ pint white wine ● ¼ pint single cream ● salt and freshly-ground pepper ● ¼ tsp grated nutmeg

Melt the butter and stir in the flour. Gradually add the stock, stirring all the time to avoid it going lumpy. (Posh Sloane cooks use a small whisk, as at La Varenne.) Add the wine and cream, still stirring. Cook until it is nicely thickened. Add seasoning and nutmeg to taste.

April

Sea trout
Like salmon, goes to sea. Returns to Scotland, etc, to spawn each year.

Brown trout
Season starts on the whole on 1st April and stops in September. Trout fishing on the chalk streams of Hampshire is the aristocrat of the sport. You have to be very skilful to present your imitation of an ephemeroptera (the small flies fish feed on) in the gin-clear water. High spot of the season – the mayfly, which appear at the beginning of June.

Rivers to fish for invitations to
Spey. Fashionable and expensive. Opens 10 February but best March–May. Tulchan (once Slater Walker's beat) might be taken for a week by Henry with two banking friends for a serious bachelor expedition. Wading up to armpits, serious risk of drowning.
Dee. Very grand – the royal fishing river, near Balmoral. February to June.
Helmsdale and *Oykel*. Smart good early-summer Scottish rivers. April–June.
Itchen and *Test*. Trout in the mayfly season. Early June.
Lough Arrow, Sligo. Trout mid-May or June. Another possible bachelor expedition.
Tweed. Boring Roller river, unusual in that it goes on fishing very late, almost best in November (season ends 31st). Enormous tube flies (serious risk of concussion from badly timed back-cast). Lower/best beats all boating at this time of year.

Other good trout rivers are: the Kennet, Avon, Nadder and smaller rivers in Devon, Cornwall, Wales, Derbyshire, Lake District, Yorkshire, Scotland.

The garden and larder

Taking stock
The smell of cut grass heralds the party season. You roll the tennis court, mow

THE TAURUS SLOANE

April 21st, enter the Taurus Sloane

The classic Taurus – dark curly hair and aggressive behaviour – hides a secret. The bull is Ferdinand – at one with nature and flowers. In short, like it or not, you're a bit of a poet, a romantic. Maybe your brain won't be preserved in aspic, but you *are* sensitive. Everyone saw you blubbing at the Royal Wedding.

You're the backbone of England at her best. You are loyal to the family and you care about appearances. You'll do up the outside of the house before you even *think* about the inside. At school they said 'Don't get middle-aged before your time' – but you went ahead and did anyway. 'Avec mes souveniers, j'ai allumé du feu.' (Only a Taurus would know that one!)

You're happy if you're healthy, and the money isn't too tight. People are always trying to change you, but you can't understand how other people can rush into things. *Your* favourite fling is a jolly house-party – masses to drink, bicycle polo, strip croquet. And no newspapers on Sunday – too intense and one-to-one.

Your secret? – You are even a bit more reactionary than you appear.

the drinks lawn and put out the croquet hoops. Croquet is always played to 'house rules', adapted to the slope of the lawn and to the family's individual skills. A visiting *champion* couldn't win.

You take stock of your garden: what is still there? Sloanes have herbaceous plants, which come up every year without you having to do anything. You have no more than two annuals, of which nicotiana (lime-green tobacco plant) is one. Sloane gardens are made up of 'boxes' (as at Sissinghurst), not rectangles (as in suburbia) or vistas (as at the Duke of Westvista's). Partitions are of stone, yew (though poison to horses) but mostly brick, to clash with the roses.

Caroline dreams of having a white and grey box (Hidcote), bog box (Savill Gardens at Windsor), white and pink rose box (Sissinghurst). Alas, she *has* a mixed border, shrubs and herbaceous, four rose beds (Superstar excluded), and Emma's box – radishes, municipal marigolds and, on Caroline's advice, nasturtiums, because they never fail and are good in nursery sandwiches.

Caroline plants crocus and snowdrop bulbs. The asparagus is starting, but asparagus isn't 'garden' to the Sloane mind – it's *social*.

At Easter, some Sloane gardens are open to the public: over 1,800 offerings big and small were in the National Gardens Scheme in 1983 (see garden in October, p 111). Sloanes are keen horticultural snoopers. You go to pry and to buy, beg or swap plants. 'This was given to me by Dini Binney/Michael Flower/Lawrence Banks.' You like things with provenance.

If *your own* garden is open, you find that visitors are interested only in: 'Where is the toilet?' or getting into the house some other way. Carolines parry enquiries from the doorway feeling like Queen Canute.

The cuckoos, warblers, swallows and swifts arrive and the conservatory is nearly finished.

Larder and freezer
Too busy with all the fresh things.

On Henry's mind

● School bills. Arrived at the end of last term and have to be paid by start of the next; and if you've got four children, that's around £4,000.
● Paying the rates.
● Make donation to school charity where Edward is sitting his Common Entrance in June. Invite housemaster to dinner. Smarm, smarm.

● Buy wine at first prices. Growers give wine merchants their opening prices towards the end of April, maybe May, and account customers can buy at the first price. You don't save much but it's fun (eg, Ch La Lagune, Médoc, 1981: opening price, £54 a case; next price, £60; Feb 1983, £69). Henry notes his wine buys down in his cellar-book (about £1.50) from Berry Bros & Rudd.
● Firm's Annual General Meeting. The chairman has a competition with his chairman friends about which can whizz the business bit through fastest at AGM. Rumours that there will be questions from a shareholder strike horror. Rumours that a director's re-election will be opposed cause blue funk.
● Old things are best, eg: *How many Sloanes does it take to change a light-bulb? Two, one to build the g & t's, the other to telephone the electrician.*
● Jamie's and Sophie's eighteenth birthday on the 19th. It is time to:
1 Buy Jamie a travelling backgammon set (Harrods, Fortnum's or similar).
2 Put him down early for an Australian visa – they're becoming hard to get (hardy Sloane boys work in Australia in the ten months between Oxbridge exams at Christmas and going up).
3 Get rid of Sophie's chunky Minnie Mouse watch – give her a small gold (plated) Seiko, £130, Atkinson.

Forward planning

★ Outfits for Ascot and other June events should be under way.
★ Do something about getting into the Cowes balls (p 87).
★ Join Epsom racecourse, if going to more than the Derby (p 69).
★ Results of the Wimbledon ticket ballot. Turn down 'restricted view' seats – not an understatement. (No warning will be given about the pigeons in the Centre Court roof – wear panama.)

MAY

Days 15 hr 40 min (av), lengthening

★ May morning madrigals from Magdalen Tower, Oxford, 1st
★ New Masters and hunt servants take over, 1st
★ May Day holiday (Sloanes hate the term Labour Day) (1984, 7th; 1985, 6th)
★ Cavalry Memorial Parade, Hyde Park, first Sunday (old and serving comrades in bowlers march from the cavalry memorial to service held beside the bandstand near Apsley House. Carolines in kit D)
★ Corso Ippico, Rome (Roman Sloanes, the Pariolini, all go, also foreign horsies like the Mark Phillipses)
★ Royal Windsor Horse Show, Wednesday to Sunday. British Driving Society's first official meet, Sunday
★ Chichester Theatre season opens
★ Perth Festival (second in Scotland to the Edinburgh F)
★ Royal Society of Portrait Painters, Carlton House Terrace (smart art. Sloanes aspire to the private view)
★ Pilgrimage to Walsingham, Norfolk (High Church and RC continuation of mediaeval pilgrimage. Duchess of Kent goes)
★ Royal Caledonian Ball, Grosvenor House (London season's reels)
★ Rose Ball, Grosvenor House (risen to the top of the deb balls)
★ Glyndebourne Opera season opens
★ Bath Festival and contemporary art fair
★ Eights Week, Oxford
★ May Week, Cambridge
★ Chelsea Flower Show, last week May (one must go – but it's how many people can you get on the head of a peony, even on Members' Tuesday)
★ Half-term around 28th
★ Royal Academy Summer Exhibition, Burlington House to Aug (private view no longer essential but you go before mid-June)
★ Late spring holiday (1984, 28th; 1985, 27th)
★ Whit Sunday (1984, 10th June; 1985, 26th May)

The polo season

Croquet for knights

March to September

Polo is a bit of a Roller sport – as Sloanes say of many things they can't afford. You get some slightly dodgy foreigners. The Argentinian problem, when all these smart brown men called Bobby disappeared from polo and became the enemy, caused a lot of heart-searching. What you like about polo is the Army-ness, the Indianness, the closeness you can get to the players and the way you see the whole game, unlike racing etc. You don't have to know a lot to know someone has scored a goal. There are four players to a team, three chukkas (periods) to a game. High-goal players are what they sound; they are the top league. Pukka, sucker, chukka, f..... –

you like the atmosphere. You feel the men are as tough as their little horses, four at least to a player.... But polo players are really in the stratosphere (cocainosphere?). Like actors: one simply does not aspire to one.

You sit beside your car, parked right up to the ropes, ogling Prince Charles and the Hipwood brothers. You'll never see HRH any closer, and Diana too – though she's obviously ill at ease. One, Charlie might fall off and break his neck. Two, his past was full of polo-going girls.

Tea in the tent is a chance to mingle, and drinks after the game another.

Watching polo – even belonging to the top clubs – is relatively cheap. Less than £60 a year gets you into a key club with a guest.

The top three clubs

CIRENCESTER PARK, Cirencester, Gloucestershire (0285 3225).
COWDRAY PARK, Midhurst, West Sussex (073 081 3257).
GUARDS', Smiths Lawn, Windsor Great Park, Englefield Green, Egham, Surrey (0784 34212).

The polo year

March
Cowdray Park and the Guards' clubs start the new season with practice games and matches.

April
Cirencester's starting date depends on the date of Badminton Horse Trials – no chukkas before Badminton is the rule.

May
The Queen's Cup at the Guards', end May to early June. The first of the major or high-goal tournaments of the British season.

June
Ascot Week Tournament at the Guards', during Royal Ascot week; play starts late so that players can rush or totter from the racecourse to the match.
Warwickshire Cup, at Cirencester, late June. Preliminary rounds are played at Cowdray and Windsor.

July
Peak polo month. British Open Championship for the Gold Cup at Cowdray, in the first two weeks of July.
International Day at Windsor on the last Sunday. This is the biggest event of the season, with typical Guards' efficiency, pomp, colour and showing off. All other clubs in the country close that day, and crowds of players, grooms, followers, etc pack the augmented stands of Smiths Lawn to watch military bands, Pony Club parades – and the polo.

September
Cowdray Park tournament.
European Polo Academy Open at the Guards'. A fairly new tournament started by German industrialist Christian Heppe. A big success and often the best weather to round off season.

Eights Week and the Mays

Blade on the feather

Late May
There's nothing more fun than the Saturday that ends the four days of the bumps at Oxford or Cambridge. The boathouses are full of Pimm's-swillers cheering their college eight as it passes ('House! House! House!' – there goes the 'House of God,' Christ Church) and the enthusiasts bumping each other along the towpath. The PA booms, whistles whistle, the Sloanes shout ('Sophie!' 'Charles – over here!'). The oars (blades) are feathering, the leaves are feathery – it's magic. The gods of the occasion, the participating oarsmen and members of the college boat clubs, wear white flannels and braided blazers, the others kit H.

You move from boathouse to boathouse with the secretaries and university girls. All are slightly sozzled, all questing friends and free Pimm's.

The trick is either to hole up in a safe Sloane enclave, such as the top of the Christ Church boathouse, or find out who has the best Pimm's and the busiest barman. With any luck he won't notice that you aren't a member of the college and the 8 pints you signed for are in a fictional non-U name. The college bars *always* lose, that's certain. It hasn't changed *that* much since Zuleika Dobson's fatal impact on the Duke of Dorset and his rivals in Eights Week, 1911.

To the oarsmen, there's something very satisfying about pursuing the boat in front until you bang it – hunting plus bumper cars. The Maggie (St John's, Cambridge) crew have red singlets and blazers and red oars. They are 'bathed in blood' because once, in the mists of history, they had a spike on their bow – until they bumped Trinity and it killed the cox. They changed the name of their boat club to Lady Margaret in penance.

During the Cambridge Mays, Maggie, First & Third Trinity, Downing, Trinity Hall and Jesus hog the top of the river year after year. In their eights you see your friends from 'the Blue Boat' in the Boat Race. The rowing fraternity at Oxford are from Oriel, Oriel, Oriel (Boriel!), Christ Church, Keble and Magdalen. Rowing men are usually 'shovers' – big chaps, six foot or more.

From Caroline's Diary

Lovely month, blossom all out, dawn chorus wakes us at 5, then 4.30! The whole countryside is having babies, including Hannah, 24 hours in labour the poor girl. Up all night, 4 puppies born, one more after caesarian, 2 dead. The caesarian boy is snuffly and weak – feeding with eye-dropper.

Henry tending his baby pheasants. Sets alarm for midnight and 3 to inspect the Rupert Brooders in case they freeze.

TROUT WITH LEMON STUFFING AND
☆ ☆ ☆ ☆ BUTTER SAUCE ☆ ☆ ☆ ☆

All Sloanes know there's nothing better than a freshly caught trout, cooked the instant it leaves the water. Why then are their freezers packed solid with the frozen version? (Answer: Henry always overdoes it.) Caroline's is now stuffed to the gills with Henry's catch. (His Papa has a rod on the Test.) The only way to treat a frozen trout, once thawed, is to stuff it, like this. (It's nice for fresh trout too.)

For 4

4 trout ● 6 tbsp soft fresh breadcrumbs ● 2 lemons ● 4 tbsp finely chopped parsley ● 4 tbsp soft butter ● salt and freshly-ground black pepper ● 4 tbsp seasoned flour ● 1–2 oz butter for frying ● 4 oz butter for sauce

Ideally, the trout should be boned and gutted from the back, leaving the head and tail on, with the belly intact. If a brutish fisherman (or fishmonger) has already slit them up the belly, fillet them and use the stuffing like a sandwich filling, between the two halves, pressing them well together.

Make the stuffing by mixing together the breadcrumbs, butter, parsley, salt, pepper and the zest of the lemons. Squeeze the lemons and moisten it with a little lemon juice, reserving the rest for the sauce.

Divide the mixture into four and stuff each fish, pressing them shut gently. Dust them in flour and fry them in butter until nicely brown on both sides. Keep them warm while you make the sauce.

Using the same pan in which you fried the fish, reduce equal amounts of lemon juice and water to half, scraping the pan juices as you do so. Add a pinch of salt and then, bit by bit, whisk in the 4 oz butter. This makes a delicious, light, creamy sauce for the fish. Don't over-heat it or it will turn oily.

'I'm a very very sharp blade'

Eights Week at Oxford: 'Heads she can walk on water'

After you score a bump, you are cheered from the boat to the boathouse. It is your finest hour; you are drunk with the admiration. You might receive the compliment of being debagged (who let those rugger buggers in anyway?) or the *ultimate* compliment of being hurled into the river by your fellow crew, wearing a firm Brideshead grin and protesting manfully. You then leap out and run, like a wet labrador, soaking the girls you pass, in pursuit of the next crew member to throw in. A token girl always gets thrown in too, eventually – usually a boisterous secretary who is drunk and chums with the crew.

A little night/water music
In the evening there are college garden cocktail parties or plays on the lawn – Shakespeare plus mosquitoes plus bad acting (your friends), but magical just the same.

If you make a bump on all four days you are set for the greatest night of your life (too bad you won't remember it). You have won a Bump Supper and an oar to hang on your wall. You and your crew mates march back to college, boat on your shoulders, cox in the boat holding the flag, all nine singing and shouting. Quick change into white flannels and rowing blazers and back to hold court in the quad with lots of champagne and longing-to-be-bumped girls. You start singing again, and climb to the top of anything handy – a gate will do, but a statue is better.

At the Bump Supper, you get the most ratted you've ever been. At Oriel, who are always head of the river (equivalent to four bumps), they burn the boat and all eight link arms and run through the fire – lots of singed eyebrows but few legs burnt away so far. It's the head of the river of your life.

That's the trouble with Sloanes. You are really like construction workers – the finest hours come before 25. Afterwards

you're a spectator, a *was*: 'He was a rowing Blue at Cambridge'. Meanwhile the swots are wearing earplugs – they'll peak at 45. Ugggh! Better a high watermark of one crowded hour of glorious life than a lifetime of watermarks in the V & A printroom.

Snow report
Melting
The season is over. The last of the chalet girls has trickled home. Many will be thinking let's piste again, as we did last winter. But will they have a good enough report from the rep to reapply in June? Most companies have report forms which are almost exactly like prep school – except that they are not sent home ('Has worked hard at French, German, Italian, Dutch and Saudi-Arabian, and progressed in both exercises and oral work. English alone leaves something to be desired').

Mid-May: the chalet girls' reunion drinks. Hooray for the piste! (spelt N E W T).

Sloanes look at paintings
Pose on your pony
The Private View Day at the Royal Academy, at the end of May, used to be the opening of the London Season, but no longer does one see a procession of Sloane kit

From Caroline's Diary

Emma will definitely end up head of the Pony Club. In her element at Windsor, wearing luminous armband and galloping around carrying messages. Alas, Prince Philip did not need her.

Ds walking through the courtyard and flowing up the stairs. There are now several private view days, swamped by the useful but so numerous Friends (£15.50 a year; OAPs, under-25s, £10).

The Private View at the Royal Society of Portrait Painters at the Mall Galleries in Carlton House Terrace (*near the Palace*) in mid-May has taken over as the social event. You wear a hat and look weddingy. Your friends are standing by their portraits. The photographers are snapping away for the glossies. The exhibition is so popular it is to be extended from two-and-a-half weeks to six. Many favourite SR artists exhibit.

Sloane galleries

Sloanes are not interested in pictures as pictures, it's what's in them. Flowers are nice, or sporting or regimental. You like the same sort of pictures on the wall as on the table-mat as on the Christmas card – well, you know, *nice* pictures.

Vernissages are few and far between, but there are two galleries whose list Caroline and all her friends are on: MALCOLM INNES, 172 Walton Street, SW3, and 67 George Street, Edinburgh. Malcie is amazing: does the Cresta, frightens St Moritz with the wail of his bagpipes, skis, runs in the London marathon, is married to a lady-in-waiting to Princess Anne. He sells modern sporting pictures: animals, birds, grouse moors. Same as: TRYON GALLERY, 23 Cork Street, W1. Actually, it's now Tryon & Moorland, but *everyone* still calls it the Tryon. (Prince Charles's friends.)

Other galleries

London: ACKERMANN, AGNEW, BURY STREET GALLERY (Lady Abdy), COL-NAGHI, MICHAEL PARKIN, PATRICK SEALE, CHRISTOPHER WOOD.
Edinburgh: CALTON GALLERY (owned by Andrew and Sarah Whitfield – very Sloane).

The tennis season
Pathetic shot, partner
Anytime the sun comes out

Sloanes are all upping their game. 'Anyone for tennis?', which for 60 years has been the catch-phrase of mickey-taking anti-Sloanes, sounds a sensible question in the Exercise Age. The polite encounters ('Good shot, partner!', 'Oh, *bad* luck') have somehow become McEnroeised ('That's the pits'. 'If you had contact lenses you could *see*'). Sloanes respond to the new tennis clothes ('Gucci running shoes!') and the harder, bright red or green surfaces (Hoorays can't fling themselves down any more in mock despair). They love fun gadgets like the Lobster, which fires practice balls ('There's one at Emma's school'), and the Ballboy, a wire basket to hold balls. They like bright yellow balls ('Fading eyesight').

The reason all these toys have appeared is that the rich and the hoi polloi are also very keen on tennis, but the Sloanes don't realise that. They still think there is a Sloane 'tennis season' (summer), when the 'game' (not sport) is used as a social asset. In Sloane terms this means an excuse for asking those Etonian brothers over – not big deals

THE ASPARAGUS SEASON

'I've never had a love affair that lasted longer than the asparagus season.'

The asparagus season *is* short and Sloanes like to keep it that way. Asparagus is hardly a *vegetable* because it's got a sex and class life of its own. Certain Sloane hostesses faced with unknowns still see asparagus as a *test*. Humorous upper-class men have been known to ask for a knife and fork . . .

The asparagus (like true Sloane love) takes 'between three and four years from seed until reaching harvesting'. The actual English Green Asparagus season runs from 15 April to 30 June, but it's normally at its best from mid-May, and the *old* asparagus is most tasty in late/mid June. You go for an asparagus which is a three-year-old male crown. (It gives Caroline a chance to mime something they rather enjoy.) You anoint the hot male crowns with melted butter, or oil-and-vinegar if cold. Not foreign muck like hollandaise.

It used to be thought that asparagus beds needed to be salted. Other pundits say asparagus beds are most productive when regularly urinated upon. Pee is important in the asparagus nitrogen cycle – it gives pee a lovely distinctive smell.

'Me, my Pimm's, my Old School tie and my old school on the Fourth of June'

P☆I☆M☆M☆'S

You *know* it's summer when the offy starts selling Pimm's again. Henry always buys No. 1 (Sloanes are very keen on brand loyalty). And did you know half the Pimm's produced each year is drunk at Henley? (favourite Sloane statistic). Oxbridge Sloanes start putting on their Pimm's uniform of striped blazers and boaters with punting poles. Barmen throughout the country dread Sloanes in the Pimm's season (it's a real pain to make individually).

For one large jug

1 part gin • 3 parts Pimm's • 6 parts White's lemonade and/or Canada Dry ginger ale • Sliced fruit: apples, oranges, lemons • Sliced cucumber (VITAL: for sandwiches and Pimm's) • Sprigs of mint and/or borage • Ice • Silver ladle • NO CHERRIES

You know you've got to play tennis this afternoon, you know it's strong, but YES PLEASE another one – it's sooo yummy. And what the hell, the sun is *actually* shining and this *is* England.

clinched on a court in mid-winter in Miami.

Henry has only recently upped his game. He used to go on to his shaly grey court in his school cricket jersey and white flannels, with bald plimsolls and a very old Dunlop Maxply Fort with equally old gut on it (it even had a Harrods stamp: they used to mark each one in the Fifties). He wasn't good (when he was at school, tennis was still a girl's game) but he was strong, and beat Jamie by battling on.

He felt he was in the respectable league of his old friend in the Temple who for fifteen years had lost in regular singles with an Oxford contemporary, but who was recently winning (his opponent had an artificial leg, but even so). Henry felt his tennis was *all right*. Then Jamie reached seventeen, and beat him. That was a black day.

Henry vs. Caroline

Henry now slogs it out with the middle-aged doubles sloggers all over his county, wielding an Arthur Ashe with V gap in the handle and wearing white shorts and Green Flash shoes. The ball suddenly disappears in the middle of play. Where *is* it? Stuck in the V in Henry's racket.

His favourite players are Evonne Cawley (Goolagong) – husband Roger is the heart-throb of players' wives – and Jimmy Connors, who used to be a problem child – a bit of a McEnroe – but age has mellowed him into a Sloane icon. Actually, Sloane families divide by age: the wrinklies like nice normal Connors, good old Jelly Bean King ('Honestly, who cares??'), and Chrissie Evert Lloyd; the children's favourite is rude McEnroe.

Caroline, who is much better than Henry, usually loses through not being so strong. Sometimes, however, her consistency wins through; she's a plonker who never misses (50 per cent of Henry's macho hard-hitters go out). She plays fairly regularly all year round with three other wives. They wear 'warm-ups' – fuzzy suit of trousers and sweatshirt ('Caroline's perspiration chemise') in pink or pale yellow or blue, by Fila or Ellesse. Her white skirt for best is too short, Henry thinks. She wears de-bobbled bobble socks (the ones that don't come over the top of the shoe – they make your legs look longer and ensure an even tan) and Gucci shoes. She has the 'geriatric's racket' – one of the big ones, a Prince. *Her* favourite players are Roger Taylor (beautiful long eyelashes) and Chrissie Evert Lloyd.

And the young
Jamie goes straight up to the net and thinks he is dominating it. 'Mine! Mine!' he calls to his partner as the ball approaches – and as it passes, 'YOURS!'. He hits everything hard, and mostly out, and throws his racket in anger a lot. He gets cross when he and Mummie lose to Henry and Sophie in a 'friendly family doubles'. Young male Sloanes are not good sports at tennis, where they discover that being a boy at a major public school does not count.

Jamie wears Fila clothes and Diadora shoes and has a Donnay racket. His favourite players are John McEnroe and Guillermo Vilas.

Emma plays a lot at school but is (just) more interested in boys and clothes than winning. To Jamie's annoyance she is the best in the family, a natural player. She wears a Florucci top or, better still, a Maggia – like Vitas Gerulaitis's – more suited to a drinks party than the tennis court and newly available in England. She has Dash shorts or a tennis skirt and a Wilson Chris Evert Lloyd Autograph. She gets bored quickly but can always remember the score. She serves quite hard the first time, safe the second. She likes to send drops, falling from a great height, and calls 'Great shot!' when Jamie puts a ball over the netting again. She gets crushes on the tennis coach when they go on holiday. Her favourite

players are Vitas Gerulaitis and Mats Wilander. There are more Mats Wilander posters on the walls of Benenden and Roedean than Constables in the whole country.

The family decided to go on a tennis holiday last Easter. For Sloanes there are *only* two places for tennis freaks to go, Marbella or the Algarve (at least at Easter). The temperature is in the mid-70s, there aren't too many undesirables, and there are plenty of other Sloanes. In Marbella you go to Los Monteros Hotel; in the Algarve, Vale do Lobo, where many Sloanes own villas and where they all congregate at Roger Taylor's place – booking via Caravela Tours, 38 Gillingham Street, SW1 (630 5366) – with legendary head pro Nick Walden, who's perfected more Sloane backhands and broken more Sloane hearts than any man since Robert Redford.

Clubs where you play
These are near London because Sloanes in other cities mainly live outside, with their own grass court or hard court, courtesy of either Henry, En-Tout-Cas or Doe.

ALL ENGLAND LAWN TENNIS AND CROQUET CLUB, Church Road, Wimbledon, SW19 (946 2244). Wimbledon. The bee's knees. If you're a member you say it's *rather* nice. Others are former champions, old aristocrats, the country's best juniors. Wonderful facilities, terribly snobby, great fun. No chance of getting in unless Daddy was a former champion or is already a member. What to other people is 'Wimbledon' is 'The Championships' to you.
ROEHAMPTON, Roehampton Lane, SW15 (876 1621). Pleasant low-key club, genteel combination of good players and social players. Less frantic socially than Hurlingham. Bit middle-aged, very safe.
ST GEORGE'S HILL, East Road, St George's Hill, Weybridge, Surrey (Weybridge 44869). The standard is pretty good here. Younger atmosphere than Roehampton though a bit stockbroker/house-plant set. Lovely plants, *nice* people, children often at arty schools like Dartington.
WENTWORTH, Wentworth Drive, Wentworth, Virginia Water, Surrey (09904 22013). Small club, overwhelmingly snob. Slap on the golf

course, the tennis is regarded by members as an extra entertainment, like Space Invaders or billiards. Members quite old – would take caddies on to the court with them if they could.

HOLLAND PARK, 1 Addison Road, W14 (603 3928). Small but fun club on Campden Hill. Beware – a bit arty.

HURLINGHAM, Ranelagh Gardens, SW6 (736 8411). Draws Sloanes from all over London, players and non-players alike. Younger, faster and slicker than the All England Club, but with a set of ruling old-timers. One Sloanette described it as 'like South Molton Street, except there's more grass'.

Sloane joke: whenever the umpire at The Championships says 'New balls, please', Hurlingham obeys. It now holds almost as many do's as Grosvenor House Hotel.

QUEEN's, W. Kensington, W14 (385 3421). The grande dame of tennis clubs. Holds the only other tournament Sloanes go to. The clubhouse is a hang-out for bridge-players, middle Europeans and deposed royalty – particularly White Russians. Not many women but some blondes. Has seen better times, and the indoor courts are much too fast for most Sloanes (you have to run).

CUMBERLAND CLUB, 25 Alvanley Gardens, NW6 (435 6022). Brand-new clubhouse, full bar and catering. A club for fairly serious tennis players – a real members' club, since there is no pro. An SDP rather than Tory haunt – 70 per cent of members from NW area.

DAVID LLOYD Slazenger Racquet Club, Southall Lane, Hounslow, Middlesex (573 0143). Very professional modern set-up: six pro instructors, high court fees, not v. Sloane. 'It's like an American racquet club,' one said. But Princess Margaret's friend Norman Lonsdale and National Hunt jockey John Francome go there (and Cliff Richard).

RACQUETS Indoor Tennis Club, Alfred Road, Westbourne Green, W2 (286 1985). Slick club for young stockbrokers, gold traders, merchant wankers. More Giorgio Armani than Harris Tweeders. Spa baths, etc.

Henry is probably also a member of a couple of other tennis things like the Bar or the Stock Exchange club. Standard is really pretty low – the idea is to go off at the weekends and play matches against the old school, the old college etc, ie have a good binge. And with luck you can even get abroad. At Cambridge the tennis players dread the arrival of the Bar – 'I've never seen anything more rah-rah in my life. The wellington boot comes to tennis!'

BAR Lawn Tennis Society, 14 Capon Close, Swaythling, Southampton.

PUBLIC SCHOOLS, Old Boys, Beech Cottage, Trodds Lane, Merror, Guildford.

STOCK EXCHANGE Lawn Tennis Club, The Stock Exchange, EC2.

Playing away

There are times when you want to play someone but not at your club – it's early days, or he's too dishy to risk, or she works for you, or he's *too* MPSIA (Minor Public School, I'm Afraid). Sloanes in this position go to Battersea, Wandsworth or Royal Hospital, Chelsea public courts. What you get up to there reaches Sloanes ears even faster than your indiscretions at Hurlingham – you forgot that Tessa Bushe-Telegraphe walks her dogs twice a day.

The opera season

A night at the opera: a lifetime of credit

Sloanes all book opera seats, whether it's Covent Garden or the Welsh or Scottish or English National or another local company. An opera-house has gilt and plush and status and top people. It is the place to take the boss, or one's Japanese

A set of young mothers and old-timers at Hurlingham

contact. When not going for such creepy reasons, Sloanes still splash out the £28–£35 necessary for the best seats. After all, the opera is a good place to meet the people you know (Caroline's letters often gush '. . . had *lovely* time at *Figaro*. We bumped into the Williamsons at the Crush Bar, haven't seen them since Glyndebourne'). Caroline thinks it an awful pity the audience doesn't wear black tie any more.

She goes to the Garden (Royal Opera House) for Puccini. She tried Wagner once. It was dreadfully long. She had had Simpson's treacle roll for lunch (a moment on the lips, forever on the hips) and by Act II of *Tristan and Isolde*, it was sitting on her stomach like a concrete bollard. When Jon Vickers dying aria was cut by hay fever, she was secretly delighted. She never could stand people who didn't go when they said they were going. And if Rossini had written that Ring Cycle, it would only have lasted two hours *and* had some jolly good tunes.

Caroline is proud to say she saw Kiri Te Kanawa as the Countess *before* the Wedding when she became the SRs' only well-known soprano. 'Dove sono' from *Marriage of Figaro* reminds Sloanes of the national anthem. At Glyndebourne Mozart is a must, especially *The Magic Flute*.

When Henry and Caroline go to Glyndebourne (near Lewes, Sussex; Ringmer 812321), he wears black tie, she wears her claret taffeta frilly. They hate going on Company nights (when sponsors have block bookings). Such an array of refurbished curtains dragging through the grass – and *coloured* dress shirts.

Henry and Caroline arrive with friends by car (helicopter is *not* acceptable) with at least one hour in hand to bag their favourite spot by the ha-ha for The Picnic. The Picnic is the focal point of Glyndebourne, as Pimm's is to

Rugalotto fun at Glyndebourne

Henley. You have picnic D, but while linen table-cloths and candelabra are admired, tables and chairs are not (you are neither French nor geriatric, and it's a long way from the car-park). Champagne or Sancerre is kept chilled in the ice-box.

The real crashing disappointment of Glyndebourne is not therefore an indisposed singer (you always applaud the replacement loudly if this does happen, for Jolly Good Show). The Worst That Can Happen is rain. Henry checks the long-range forecast and books up at Wallop Halls (a picnic in the car absolutely kills the spirit of the thing and the marquee is too like the village fête).

The other Sloanopera trip is a long weekend at the end of October at Wexford: three v. obscure operas on twelve days in the Theatre Royal (Wexford 22240). Henry and Caroline don't know the operas but the people are much nicer than those at the Edinburgh Festival. They get tickets and quickly book at White's or the Talbot, the two hotels in Wexford (those Anglo-Irish mansions are so draughty). You remember to take warm waterproof clothing (you know *Ireland*), plus evening dress.

The day starts late, at lunchtime. Henry and Caroline take in a few exhibitions in the afternoon.

But the real fun is in the evening. The last performance of the festival is the best, when they announce which operas have been chosen for next year. You clap like mad even though you haven't heard of those three either.

If you're feeling peckish you visit the jolly festival oyster bar (one customer remarked that he'd never appreciated smoked salmon more than after *Of Mice and Men*). Then it's back to the hotel bar until the early hours, where Bernard Levin is holding court in a corner. Even

Henry is surprised how much the Irish drink. But a Sloane simply can't *resist* competition.

The punting season

Prowess with the pole
From May through the summer
Seriously social Oxford and Cambridge Sloanes go up before term starts. They can be seen punting along the river so as to be pole-perfect later, when they have girls aboard. At Oxford they stand at the Oxford, ie 'right' end – the slatted, sloping end – and are very scornful of anyone who uses the Cambridge, wrong, end – where it's flat. They always try to get a wooden pole. (The aluminium poles are vulgar and make a horrid ringing noise when they strike bottom. Aluminium *is* a light vulgar metal.)

There are various riverside pubs in Cambridge (and Grantchester for tea)

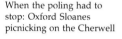

When the poling had to stop: Oxford Sloanes picnicking on the Cherwell

THE GEMINI SLOANE

May 22nd, enter the Gemini Sloane

People are always telling you you're terribly attractive and vivacious. The Gemini Sloane *does* talk nineteen to the dozen – but then you have to make up for the fact that other people are *so* slow. And you are a bit of a flirt. The converse of this is that depression has a habit of catching up with you; your alter ego is a moody one. Still, nobody's perfect.

For a Sloane, you can't be bothered with too much tradition. You like making your own though – a party held a certain time every year, a special drink which *everyone* associates with you. But you don't like being pinned down, and can be a bit naughty about leaving the boss – or the house – in the lurch. You seem to spend your life making tea for removal men.

You're not a madly family person. Poor Henry can go for days on cheese and biscuits in the evening ('but he eats those *large* lunches') and the freezer is well-stocked with fish fingers for the children ('The children *adore* them'). Mummie is *always* nagging you about forgetting the parrot's or the hamster's birthday ('But if you love someone, you shouldn't have to keep proving it all the time'). But they all seem to thrive on it – you encourage people to look after themselves and *be* themselves.

Your secret: Perhaps you're just a little bit selfish.

From Caroline's Diary

Staying at the flat for Chelsea. Peaceful and beautiful, 8 to 10, despite irksome one-ways, and was just getting some tips from Beth Chatto when suddenly in poured everyone, including Jane who had driven up. It was like a rugger scrum. Lunch Le Perroquet at the Berkeley with Z – every single soul we knew stuffing themselves with anchovies – then to Christopher Wood's Victorian flower pictures p.view.

Rushed home to my tiny animals and preparations for the galumphers' half-term. Hannah hates to leave puppies for a minute, eats their little messes. They're adorable, blind and squeaking.

---

but in Oxford the only Sloane punt-stops are the Cherwell Boathouse (for dinner) and the Vicky Arms (Victoria Arms). After several pints, you hijack other Sloane punts or steal their poles. One group of Hoorays were so exhilarated they decided to have a swim. They stripped to their Marks & Sparks boxers and set off splashing upstream, straight into *Three Men in a Boat*: the bloated corpse of a calf, legs in the air, had come down on the current to join them.

The garden and larder

Heaven (on earth)

The roses are beaded with greenfly because Caroline doesn't like pesticides. Luckily Henry is a chemical-killer addict.

Time to empty, scrub and refill the pool: the water takes at least three weeks to warm up. 'Sailors say the two happiest days of a yachtsman's life are the day he buys his boat and the day he sells it,' says Henry, scrubbing away. 'For boat, read swimming pool.'

On top of the work, the cost of the chemicals to keep it clean makes your eyes water. And a few hot days will bring invasion by armies of persons you barely consider acquaintances. Genghis Khan had nothing on the ruthlessness of parents whose children want a swim. One Shire Sloane deliberately keeps his pool cold and dirty primarily to discourage his in-laws. This is partly because, like many Sloanes who own a pool, he considers his gin to be part of its equipment. The rich are never under this illusion.

. The azaleas are looking fine, especially the white Palestrina. You start to thin the gooseberries, and dead-head lilac, rhododendrons and azaleas as they finish flowering. You see that the ground elder has smothered the periwinkle, the opposite of what you intended. Meanwhile Jack mows the lawn with the Ransome: Henry *must* have stripes.

Caroline rewards herself as usual with Members' Day at the Chelsea Flower Show. She makes an early appearance in the tent, neat in kit C. She collects masses of catalogues, and later orders unsuitable exotic plants which, like hats, only live one season.

Back in the garden, she keeps finding pathetic naked fledglings. She has learnt not to kill these by overfeeding, and offers half a meal-worm or some boiled egg.

Freezer and larder

Apart from Henry's fish – coming in in a steady trickle – everything's too young to store. Oh God, make me provident but not yet.

On Henry's mind

● Getting one's about-to-graduate god-son a job. Young Tim's been trying hard since the New Year. He's been turned down by ICI, Shell and Unilever. God-father Sloane telephones City friends in May – the City is after all one of the few areas of British life to pay on a European wage scale. (Henry understands that credit is not limitless, so he doesn't pull his *biggest* string – that's for Jamie.) He replenishes his favours credit when he can: with a day's good shooting, a tip from the trainer's mouth, lending workhorse Caroline to the charity and of course, opera seats – the top person's credit deposit.

● Job evaluations. Employees write these, then the boss's rating of him/her follows in June and the rise starts 1 July (– only creeps always get them). Henry and those lower down the scale write brilliant new chapters for the novel, full of 'responsibility for . . . leading to the continued success of the firm . . .' (chooses the whisky and claret for big clients at Christmas); 'report directly to

. . .' (don't tell him, but regale the Hoorays over liquid lunch in the Jam-pot); 'maintain the firm's contacts around the world' (use the office telephone whenever you're alone to tell friends in Verbier/Sydney/Hong Kong/ Boston/Honolulu about last night's party).

Forward planning

★ Wexford priority booking for Friends of the Wexford Festival Opera at begin-ning of May, remaining tickets on sale from June.

★ Beginning of next month, organise Henley vouchers (p 75).

JUNE

Days 16 hr 31 min (av).
High point of the year

★ Royal Bath and West Show, Shepton Mallet, first week (farming and landowning Sloanes)
★ Epsom summer meeting, first week. Derby, Wed; Coronation Cup, Thurs; Oaks, Saturday
★ 4th of June at Eton, Saturday nearest the 4th
★ Midsummer Ball, Hopetoun House, Edinburgh, for Prince's Trust (weeks before 24th)
★ O-level and A-level X-ams, 6th–29th
★ Common Entrance for some birthdays
★ Bookrest Ball, Hurlingham, Wednesday
★ Ski Club Ball, Hurlingham, Friday
★ South of England Agricultural Show, Ardingly, Sussex, including hound show
★ Grosvenor House Antiques Fair
★ The Queen's official birthday, Saturday: Trooping the Colour (1984, 9th; 1985, 8th)
★ Birthday Honours list in *The Times* and *Daily Telegraph* ('If Henry refuses to get himself knighted I'll have to become a Dame')
★ Prince Philip's birthday, 10th (b 1921)
★ Aldeburgh music festival opens, for two weeks
★ Oxford v Cambridge shooting match, Holland & Holland, Northwood
★ Ramadan begins (Henrys with Gulf biz sympathise with Ari Al-Sloan's fast)

★ Royal Ascot race meeting, Tuesday to Friday
★ Ascot Week Guards' Polo Club Tournament, Windsor: same dates plus weekend
★ Other polo at Cirencester, Cowdray, Windsor
★ British Driving Society show, Windsor
★ Test Match/Oxford v Cambridge at cricket (these matches often clash)
★ Longest day, 21st: Prince William's birthday (b 1982)
★ Midsummer Day, 24th
★ Irish Derby, the Curragh, Dublin, Saturday nearest Midsummer Day (many Sloanes go over to join the O'Sloanes and McGrafia, particularly when the English Derby winner is trying for the double)
★ University finals
★ Oxford Commem and summer Balls
★ Cambridge May Balls
★ University year ends
★ Passing-Out Parade and ball, Sandhurst
★ Royal Highland Show, Ingliston, Edinburgh (starts the Scottish mini-season)
★ Wimbledon fortnight, Monday mid-June to first Sunday in July
★ Parents' Day and Sports Day at schools
★ Royal Garden Party, Holyroodhouse Palace, Edinburgh, Wednesday
★ Henley Royal Regatta, last Thursday in June to first Sunday in July
★ Leander Ball, Leander Club, Henley, Saturday

Snow report
First light fall of chalet girls
The official start of the Sloane skiing year (June to May). In June, keen Sloane girls apply to be chalet girls the following season, brandishing diplomas from Winkfield and Tante Marie – and references ('Amanda . . . mainstay of this wine bar . . .'). You can apply up to September, but the earlier the better chance of a good resort.
Top employers
BLADON LINES, 309 Brompton Road, SW3 (581 4861)
JOHN MORGAN, Meon House, Petersfield (0730 68411)

(Bought in April 1983 by the worryingly unSloane Meon Travel. Are they on the slippery slope? Wait and ski. . . .)
SUPERTRAVEL, 22 Hans Place, SW1 (584 5060)

Division 2
SKI MACG, 26a Fulham Road, SW10 (351 5446)
SKI 3-V, Thackeray Street, W8 (938 1481)
SKI VAL, 91 Wembley Park Drive, Wembley, Middlesex (200 6080)
SKI WEST, Westfield House, Westbury, Wilts (0373 864811)
SNOWTIME, 122 Charing Cross Road, WC2 (836 3237)

Jamie and his pals go for it. The Fourth of June is very coeducational

Chalet girls rendezvous with their punters – past and prospective – at the Ski Club of Great Britain Ball. It's everyone's chance to see what the other half looks like out of salopettes and moon boots.

The Fourth of June

Eton and drinking
Saturday nearest 4 June

The overweening fame of Eton irritates the other public schools ('Media types for media hypes'), but Founder's Day (George III's birthday) has become something Old Boys of all schools feel they should have been to. Girls notch up their invitations beside their Oxbridge Ball tally. You should be accompanied by an Old or serving Etonian, but one has seen unaccompanied pushy people who have no connection at all. . . .

The weather is always glorious – influence. From noon, about 7,000 cars gather on Agar's Plough around the cricket pitch (the Eleven are playing the Old Boys, but who cares?). The boys are allowed to wear buttonholes with their tails and the town flower-sellers were out early with carnations of every colour including dyed Eton turquoise.

If you are serious, you visit your son's housemaster or listen to Sixth Form Select reciting literature in knee-breeches. But if you came for the picnic, you spread it out on the grass (picnic D minus table). You wander round between courses, glass in hand, meeting friends and mixing hangovers to the 'British Grenadiers' from the band. Divorcees avoid each other – and the *steps*. Some inhibited Sloanes are shocked (and secretly excited) at seeing *that* Norman family best friends with *that* millionaire Jewish advertising man. The whole thing is the oddest mixture of the past (the buildings, the events) and new

June

striped shirts though. Several Sophies, eighteenth-century visions in Laura Ashley, have come with last year's Old Boys. About 20 turn up on motor bikes with girls and roar round chewing up the grass and making a din. There is a hired bus of Bullingdon drunks from Oxford, a minibus from Cambridge (exam time), a dry bus from Wycombe Abbey and a dry bus from Winkfield. St Mary's Wantage came in a bus one year but have not been allowed to venture since.

The school frowns on the drinking because of the fighting. After a few Pimm's, the loathesomeness of the re-encountered bully or swot or creep inflames you. A job and a wife have compounded his crime. There is *always* a fathers' fight. Two mothers even fought, swinging their handbags, after one returned to the shared picnic to find that the other's sons had Eton all the strawberries.

If you don't catch one of these bouts, there is always the Procession of Boats after 3. You troop to the riverbank, the band starts the 'Eton Boating Song' and the first boat appears round the corner below Windsor Castle. The crews of the

money and power. Famous parents ogle film-star cars, and the *incredible* girls – punked-up sisters and Koo Stark-types – big brothers' big game. The Fourth of June is much more like St Tropez than a Sloane ghetto event.

Henry and Caroline are in kit H. Lots of other fathers wear straight suits and

Letter from Charlie (Dragon School) to Edward (Cheam)

Dear Ed (or are ya Harold today?)

How are you? I am OK I suppose. Too much Latin, not enough butterscotch whip, you know.

Just got back from Fathers' Match (GROAN). I had to play against the Tyrant who was wearing <u>flares</u> (YUK!). He was in a real raz with me because I dropped two catches from Smith's dad's bat. Smith's dad used to play for Warwickshire 2nd eleven. Does he want a crippled son? The Tyrant drank so much whisky at lunch he was run out (HA HA!). I was out LBW for nine. I am having a bad season like Ian Botham. Smith's father did something to his back. I don't think old people should play cricket.

They came in the Renault!! That spaz Fielding Minor said his parents owned a Porsche and then

they turned up in a yukky yellow Ford!!! So I felt a bit better.

Our food is getting more disgusting by the minute. Cook has hay fever and gone AWOL. If I have one more ham salad I shall go BONKERS. This place gets more like a concentration camp every day. I asked the Tyrant if I could go to Holland Park. He said that it was not the place for the likes of us and the only reason Nigel went there was because his parents are Communists. I said they voted Labour but he says it's the same thing, no moral fibre.

Anyway I have to do my Geog prep now. Could you video Top of the Pops for me? I have been banned from the TV room again. Mr Thompson has <u>no</u> sense of humour.

See ya
Chas

eights wear nineteenth-century naval uniforms and flower-decked boaters. They're all future Cabinet ministers and bank directors. This is what is meant by the flowering of English manhood.

As they pass, the rowers lift their oars in pairs and rise unsteadily to their feet. When all the crew are standing, they raise their hats to Windsor and to Eton, shaking the flowers into the water. The spectators pray someone will fall in or a boat sink. Alas, they simply blade away.

It's about time for you to leave now. Jamie attends roll-call ('Absence') in School Yard. 'Here' – then he's free to be not here, for half-term. Departing, young Sloanes become most belligerent, roaring round in their cars and addressing strangers: 'You absolute shit! Which school did you go to? I bet it was Harrow. Bloody *Harrow*.'

One social editor (not *Harpers & Queen*'s), who had gone to sleep under a car, woke up in the dark to find himself alone in the field. The 7,000 had fled.

The Derby

Black top hat for Tattenham Corner
First Wednesday in June
The most-prestige flat race of all (never mind the £250,000 prize money). A stud value of at least £10 million descends on a stallion as he crosses the finishing line.

The largest traffic jam in southern England forms early at Epsom on Derby Day (gate open at 10). In it is a Sloane bus, hired by Sophie, who organises friends, picnic, *crates* of champoo (charging about £9 a head), to start at some hub of the universe like Battersea. You hear the helicopters of the swanky classes spluttering overhead (Hascome Aviation Services of Bishop's Stortford run them from London heliport).

Henry is a member at Epsom, £50 plus £26 for each of two guests he's allowed to bring. He joined in April so as to get in the whole year's racing (nine days) –

(United Racecourses, Racecourse Paddock, Epsom, Surrey; 03727 26311).

The less said about the lavatories the better, but nothing – not even the National – can produce such a sense of occasion. Adrenalin joins the Bollinger in Henry's bloodstream. Will his horse get round Tattenham Corner (see p 42)? Caroline is more worried about her dress and hat – not as dressy as Ascot, but not something seen before. It's no good following the Queen – her Derby dresses are a disaster.

Henry is in sensible black morning suit and silk hat – he and Caroline are guests in the Owners' and Trainers' enclosure. He moves between this, the members' tent and his firm's tent or box (lobsters, strawbugs and champers). Or they might bring a picnic (members' car-park ticket, £8).

It was at the Derby that the nation found out for sure that the Queen bets. (A friend places the bets for her.) When Psidium won at 66 to 1 in 1961, a photographer caught her with Punter's Agony all over her face. Henry knows.

Ascot

It's certainly not racing
Tuesday to Friday, mid-June
Royal Ascot brings the Sloane family together, like Christmas. Henry and Caroline's parents wouldn't miss it any more than they would, any more than

The Procession of Boats. 'We'll sink, sink together, and swear at the best of schools'

Racing umbrellas with pencils to mark one's card

June

Sophie would. *She*'s got to be seen by her fellow eighteens. It takes place the week of the Waterloo dinner at Windsor, and the Queen comes every day.

This year, Henry and Caroline feel that Jamie is old enough. In March, he writes to Her Majesty's Representative, Ascot Office, St James's Palace, SW1. His letter reads: 'James Sloane (17) presents his compliments to Her Majesty's Representative and begs the honour of a special voucher for the enclosure at Ascot. (This is a first application.)'

The Ascot Office sends him a form. He fills it in, and has it signed by a sponsor (Henry), who must have been to the Royal Enclosure four times. First-time applicants must apply before 31 March. People who have been before must apply before the end of April. Start applying from 1 January: if there are too many applicants for Gold Cup day, Thursday, the names are put in a ballot. The Royal Enclosure was £48 in 1983 for the four days, or £20 a day, half-price for 16 to 25-year-olds; more in 1984. Divorced people may go now, since Queen Mary handed in her veto. Henry says it's *too* bad: it would be lovely and empty without them.

You each receive a non-transferable voucher, which you exchange for a badge at the office outside the enclosure on the day. Next day, you hand in the first badge and get a new one. It's uncrashable. No danger of hitting the POWess with the prole.

In the three-mile jam converging on Ascot you inspect the other Sloane cars with hats squashed into the rear windowsill. You park in No 1 car-park, the most social. But you have to book in July the year before to be sure (over £12 for the four days; Grandstand Office, Ascot Racecourse, Ascot, Berks; 0990 22211). But there are four other car-parks for the Royal Enclosure mob, so don't panic.

You settle down to summer picnic D (table), champagne – the works. You avoid the Ascot restaurant – rather non-U. Everyone's looking incredibly smart in kit J. The rule is morning dress or national dress. As Jamie couldn't borrow his father's or grandfather's, he hired one – a long time in advance – from Moss Bros, where he refused to be fobbed off with grey. You do *not* hire grey ones. The hired polloi look *absolOOTli* dreadful in their ill-fitting grey suits.

The Prince and Princess of Wales at Ascot. Supersloane moves like a thoroughbred

*Godfatherly
invitation to watch
Trooping the Colour
from the Cabinet
office. Better picture
on the telly than from
the window, but felt
very privileged. Wine
served by liveried
flunkeys, and H and
I kept trying to lean
out of the window
with our glasses, but
this a FATAL
mistake – shadows of
armed detectives on
the roof, the high-
powered guns looking
terrifyingly much
larger in silhouette.*

Henry has brought his umbrella, because a) NO macs, and b) there's always a downpour. Caroline wears a different dress every day, hat (the rule) and gloves. But she never *over*dresses, least of all on Ladies' Day, Thursday, when that OTT Mrs Shilling and the noovos appear in the most vulgar hats and ridiculous long Edwardian evening dresses which they claim belonged to their grandmothers (as if they *had* grand-mothers). Their husbands used to wear *brown* morning suits, and some Sloanes stay away from Ladies' Day with shrieks of 'Brown shoes and brown bowlers!' The poor Queen, she *has* to go.

Lunch must be finished by two, so as to see HM driving in from Windsor and along the racecourse in her carriage. There's always a good turn-out from Windsor in the royal procession.

Jamie sneaks off to the bookies after inspecting the debs. It's useful that everyone has their names on their lapels.

Henry, as a serious racegoer, secretly dislikes Ascot: he resents his pitch being invaded by Sloane males not normally seen on racecourses but now dressed up as though *they* were as interesting as horse- or girl-flesh – literally wagging their tails. Henry does not talk to such persons even if known.

In the evening, the streets of Ken-sington are full of People Like You in morning dress. Sloane solidarity. Even the noovos look OK in the half-light.

May Balls/Commem Balls

More prowess with the pole
Mid-June
Cambridge college balls are called May Balls although they are held in June. Initiates all know that. The best are Tri-nity, Magdalene and Pembroke (King's is decreasingly Sloane).

In Oxford there is one Commem Ball a year, held in rotation by Christ Church, New College or Magdalen. The best of the other summer balls are Worcester (for the garden and lake) and Oriel.

Undesirables ('Who let *them* in?') are deterred by the high prices (say, £80 for a double ticket) and by the fact that the tickets are not offered for sale to the public: if you want one, you need a friend in the college to buy it.

For many Sloanes, however, gate-crashing is half the fun. It's difficult, because ball committees spend a large proportion of their budget on security guards, but nothing beats the thrill of hanging from a rope in the darkness with an Alsatian snapping at your feet (corps training from school comes in useful here) – except, that is, telling your friends about it afterwards.

Dress is black tie, though at Mag-dalene and Trinity, Cambridge, you wear white (and if you're in the Bullingdon Club, the most feared crowd in Oxford, you wear turquoise – 'Who let *that* in?'). There are usually two sittings for dinner, one at around nine o'clock and another at midnight. Most people try to book the first. If you turn up late, you could find yourself sitting on the floor eating chicken salad from a plastic pack. ('This is no *ordinary* drumstick, this is a £40 drumstick.')

Over dinner you study the programme. This needs brainpower, because there are several events on at the same time – a band, a disco, a film, a snake-charmer. You end up missing half of them (cabarets are particularly hard to get into). Muscly Sloanes lift their girlfriends on to their shoulders for a better view, enjoying the annoyance which this causes the people behind them.

You trek round and round relent-lessly, quad to quad, marquee to mar-quee, until it's time for breakfast (disappointingly small and froggy: a cup of coffee and a roll).

June

At dawn, you prize open your eyelids, grab another bottle, and take up position for the survivors' photograph.

By now, you are probably experiencing the Sloane's high, which comes after six hours of some strenuous open-air activity, helped by libations of alcohol. Dawn on the lawn at an Oxford or Cambridge ball then suddenly flowers into this wonderful secret state. Sloanes *are* spiritual, but in their own way.

In Cambridge (superior to Oxford in having the colleges actually *on* the river) figures in evening dress punt along the Backs under the spotlit trees. Cambridge balls are larger than Oxford ones, and attended by a surprising number of older Sloanes. ('Will they let *me* in when I'm 84?')

The Sloane wedding

Organising the wedding
This begins *months* in advance. The invitations have to be ordered (wedding minus three months), then sent (W −2). The dress for the bride, and those of the supporting cast, must be chosen or made (W −3); the reception arranged, with all its ingredients: food, flowers, champagne, help (W −4), and perhaps hotel (W −6); and, of course, the church (W −5). You feel a bit of a fraud visiting your local vicar, whose establishment you have patronised for only two out of the last 52 Sundays (thank goodness for Mummie's church drudgery). But getting married in one of the London wedding churches such as St Michael's, Chester Square or Holy Trinity, Brompton, involves even more cynicism. There are three times as many spinsters-of-this-parish married in the smart churches as *exist*. But you attend to hear your banns read, and you *are* sincere in wanting God's help in the enterprise of living with Simon.

Be upstanding for the speech of the best man
Time may ring the changes among certain Sloane customs, but June still rhymes with moon, drunken loon and bridegroom. The wedding is when the best – and the worst – of Sloaneness is on show, like the wedding presents, for all the world to see. And hear.

Unfortunately there is no joke book to keep young Sloane best men on the rails. But they have their own little manure heap, published here for the first time.

'I remember well our days at university . . . we were so poor in those days . . . in fact, Simon's digs were the only ones where the dustmen used to deliver. . . .'

'At school he was not the most popular boy. We used to call him Hanky, because he got up everyone's noses. . . .'

'. . . on sports day, he got the job of catching the javelin. . . .'

'Bride's bouquet *up* a few inches, groom's parents' hands on pages' shoulders – no, don't strangle him – close in a little, and all *smile*'

Nightmares with the house-parties and last-minute preparations for the wedding and dance. Annabel tearing round like a mad thing. I warned her not to cry, if she didn't want to look like a boiled owl.

Then the night before, John said the inevitable. 'My poor little Bella, leaving her Daddy for another man' – floods of tears, a pair of boiled owls. Then he asked if she was doing the right thing – after all these house-parties and arrangements! The callousness of the man!!

All over. Feel so THANKFUL but have no clear picture. Worried myself into a passionless daze. H red in the face and smiling at no one, Eliz lips trembling, Annabel beautiful but her bouquet shaking.

Best man's speech the most off-key I've ever heard. Even H thought he went a bit far about the new member of the family. He'll probably end up Lord Mayor.

Dance a success. Men and girls drank too much and shrieked into the night. Silk jacket, cigarette packets, crushed plants, a girl's shoe discovered round the garden next day.

Annabel and Simon appeared again, and went away for good about midnight – a gush of boiled owl again, but Simon gallantly rang next morning to say she'd stopped. Sophie must get married in a registry office. I may recover in time for Emma's.

ICED CHICKEN WITH LEMON SAUCE

PANIC! Caroline has volunteered to make ten people's dinners for a fund-raising banquet (tickets £17.50 each and 250 guests expected). All the cooks have been given exactly the same recipes (Water Lily Timbale, Iced Chicken with Lemon Sauce, Chocolate Mousse) but everyone knows they'll all come out looking completely different. Will Caroline's offering match the elegance of Lucy's? or Annabel's? or Venetia's? This is the chicken recipe, a close relation of Constance Spry's Coronation Chicken (b. 1953), of which some unconventional Sloanes are beginning to tire.

For 10

2 3½–4 lb chickens ● 1 onion and a bouquet garni ● 2 oz butter ● 2 tbsp flour ● 1½ pts chicken stock (reserved from poaching the chicken) ● salt and pepper ● 1 lemon, its rind grated and juice squeezed out ● 4 egg yolks ● 1 pint single cream ● parsley sprigs

Poach the chickens in water to which you have added an onion, their giblets, bouquet garni and salt. When they are tender, drain them and leave them to get cold. Reserve 1½ pints of their stock for the sauce. Remove the skin and bones from the chickens and cut them into neat pieces. Arrange them in a serving dish.

To make the sauce, melt the butter and stir in the flour. Gradually add the stock, stirring to make a smooth sauce and to avoid lumps. Add the lemon rind, lemon juice, salt and pepper. Remove from heat. Beat the egg yolks with the cream and add a ladle or two of the sauce. Mix well and return this liaison to the sauce. Heat it gently again, without boiling. Allow it to cool to lukewarm, then spoon it over the chicken. Cover and chill in the fridge. Decorate with sprigs of parsley for serving.

'He's the only man I know who gets threatening telephone calls from the Samaritans. . . .'

'I found him one day making obscene calls to the speaking clock.'

'If we gave Simon a pound for every woman he's had, there'd be enough to buy him a small sherry. . . .'

'But Simon's a good catch. His teeth are all his own – he showed me the receipt; and his hair is all real – not *his*, but it's real. . . .'

'Let's leave the old days behind . . . This is meant to be a happy occasion – despite this speech . . . Simon always wanted to grow up and be an accountant – he's achieved one of those ambitions . . . Then he met Annabel. Annabel's a remarkable girl; she used to have a foot fetish, but she's settled for eight or nine inches. . . .'

Caterers and planners for parties and weddings

SEARCY TANSLEY & CO, 136 Brompton Road, SW3 and 30 Pavilion Road, SW1 (584 3344) is the great name in Sloane catering.

PARTY PLANNERS'. Lady Elizabeth Anson (a cousin of the Queen's), 56 Ladbroke Grove, W11 (229 9666) will plan the whole party/wedding for you, including sending out the invitations.

Country

JEAN ALEXANDER, Great Goodwin Farm House, Old Merrow Street, Merrow, Guildford, Surrey (Guildford 71326)
ROBIN BRACKENBURY, Holme Pierrepont Hall, Holme Pierrepont, Nottingham (Radcliffe-on-Trent 2371)
MISS SARAH JAGGARD, Drewetts. Butlers Leap, Rugby, Warwickshire (Rugby 4171, 76915)
THE KIMPTON KITCHEN, Fernhurst, Haslemere, Surrey (Haslemere 52043)
BRIDGETT MAUDE, Chestnut Farm, Drayton Parslow, Milton Keynes,

Buckinghamshire (Mursley 262)
NADDER CATERING (Peter Combes), Manor Farm House, Dinton, Nr Salisbury, Wiltshire (Teffont 495)
WILLIAM'S KITCHEN, 3 Fountain Street, Nailsworth, Gloucestershire (Nailsworth 2240)

Scotland

D. S. CRAWFORD, 19 Elbe Street, Edinburgh (Edinburgh 554 6651)
MRS RODERICK I'ANSON, Montague House, Balbeggie, Perthshire (Balbeggie 363)
OPEN ARMS HOTEL, Dirleton, East Lothian (Dirleton 241)
MRS JOHN WILSON, Country Kitchen, Heron's Court, Killearn, nr Glasgow (Killearn 50286)

The flowers

The great names are:
PULBROOK & GOULD, 181 Sloane Street, SW1 (235 3186)
(Lady Pulbrook gets her flowers from country gardens). The other great

London names are:
MOYSES STEVENS, Lansdowne House, Berkeley Square, W1 (493 8171)
CONSTANCE SPRY, 53 Marylebone Lane, W1 (486 6441)

Country

MRS ANTONY BUTTERWICK, Pinkneys House, Pinkneys Green, Maidenhead, Berkshire (Maidenhead 21726). Works with:
MRS LOUDON CONSTANTINE, The Old Rectory, Amersham, Buckinghamshire (Amersham 7475)
MARGARET FERGUSON, Pirbright Lodge, Pirbright, Surrey (Brookwood 2171)
JANIE HEYNES, Newton Lodge, nr Farringdon, Oxon (Buckland 225)
MRS COLIN TANGYE, Littlefield Manor, Worplesdon, Surrey (Worplesdon 232076)

Scotland

FAIR CITY FLOWERS, 54 George Street, Perth (Perth 24299)
LADY MACMILLAN, Finlaystone, Langbank, Renfrewshire (Langbank 235)

Wimbledon

Something in the way he moves ...

Monday mid-June to first Sunday in July
Wimbledon (Windlebum, Henry calls it) is a Sloane must, and you really indulge yourself about fancying the players: in fact if you don't you pretend to (as with Derby runners). Feeling physical about one of the Wimbledon players is de rigueur for Sloanes from 15 to 55.

Caroline spends hours in front of the box. She and Henry actually go once or twice, Caroline in dress, sunglasses, hat if un-covered stand, Henry in grey flannels and panama. They got tickets because they sent off between 1 October and the end of January for an application form (All England Lawn Tennis Club, Church Road, Wimbledon, SW19. Enclose an sae). Their application, with the rest of the 100,000, was then put in a ballot for the Centre and No 1 courts. (People unlucky in the ballot go on the list for cancellations, so if you missed the ballot, you won't get tickets.)

There are 400 unreserved tickets a day for the Centre and No 1 courts, except for the last four days – but you hate queueing: and all those sweaty students with their sleeping-bags. If you didn't get a ticket, you go in the first week and pay at the turnstiles – Monday and Wednesday are good to see the male stars on the outer courts. Like everyone else, you prefer men's tennis.

You *wish* you could get into the plush enclosure for members and players. Sloanes throw the word 'debenture-holder' (stockholder in the All-England Club) around grandly – Henry's uncle is one, but he only gets one ticket a day for his stock and he had to pay £3,000 for it. It's sold every five years on the Stock Exchange: next chance, 1985.

Many a young Sloane string-pulls a job at Wimbledon (especially undergraduates, 'to earn a bit of cash before going to the Far East'). One Sloane girl got the job of changing the score on the Centre Court, pre-digital, and was forever putting up the wrong one after too much wine in the debenture lounge.

Young Sloanes go star-spotting at Alexander's, 138a King's Road, SW3 (584 4604). A restaurant run by playboy José and his wonderful wife Amanda, it is *the* tennis hang-out and McEnroe's winning racket is on the wall.

You can't go to the finals, because they inevitably clash either with Henley or Sophie's sports day. You take the portable television and flicker your eyes from boats to Sarah Arche-Ryvell's hat to the housemaster to Navrat to Sophie like a demented ant, as Sloanes say.

Henley
What does rowing matter;
hats in the breeze
Last Thursday in June to first Sunday in July
Henley Royal Regatta is the Wimbledon of rowing (and, maddeningly, clashes with the Wimbledon finals – but the tennis score is announced over the Tannoy). Henley is not the most important international event any more, but it is certainly still the prettiest, with the boats racing two-by-two along a straight stretch of the upper Thames below a backdrop of trees and hillside. The log-jam of boats beside the course is reminis-

Hooray Henleys in the Bridge Bar: 'Wah wah wah wah'

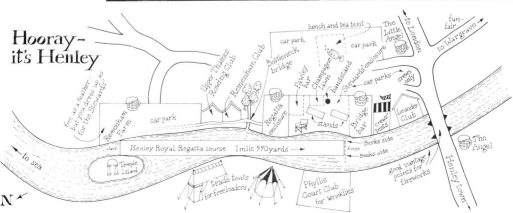

Hooray – it's Henley

cent of Macao, except for the shape of the hats. Never (not since last year) have so many bowls of strawberries and cream been passed so precariously through so many hands down so many rocking little boats.

The racing offers eights, single sculls, fours, pairs; school, university and international oarsmen. 'We're all queers together, that's why we go round in pairs', as one parody of the Eton Boating Song goes. But the keen are outnumbered here as usual. *Most* people have come to watch each other. They think the pink blazer of Leander, British rowing's Holy of Holies (club house 100 yards from the finish) is hideous – *and* the pink socks and the hippo motif.

Leander used to be exclusive (oarsmen only), but there is now an associate membership, open to all *except* women. But most Sloanes still go to the Stewards' Enclosure opposite the finish, though that takes planning. You have to be a member, a member's guest, or get a member to sign a voucher for you. You can either send off the signed voucher or present it at the gate and pay the daily rate. In 1983, this was £7 for Thursday, £10 Friday, £13 Saturday, £10 Sunday. You can get the voucher signed at any time before the regatta – there is no closing date. But there is a quota each day, so you can't arrive too late. Racing starts at 9 on Thursday, 9.45 on Friday, 10 on Saturday and 12 on Sunday.

To become a member of the Stewards' Enclosure, two members have to propose and second you. The Secretary, Henley Royal Regatta, Regatta House, Henley-on-Thames (04912 2153) has a very nice and helpful staff. You have priority if you have rowed, or married a rower, or something else bladey.

A member gets a ticket for himself each day, two extras for Thursday and Friday, one extra on Saturday and Sunday. It is well worth the annual subscription (£35) if you like to take guests. Initial

membership is £50 unless you are a past competitor, when it is much less.

Everyone dresses for the Stewards' Enclosure. Kit H for men, Caroline in hat and floaty pastel dress. Aged and pear-shaped Sloanes blazon their youthful sporting prowess with faded school blazers from the back of the cupboard. No jeans allowed, no girls in trousers, culottes or minis (any skirt above the knee). One Rangerette in culottes who was turned away came back with both legs squeezed down one side of the garment. Every year a few people get thrown in for crimes against propriety. Only once has the stiff upper lip relaxed (lip on the quiver, rot on the breeze): in the Great Drought Year, 1976, on the Saturday afternoon, when it was 90 in the shade. Gentlemen were 'permitted to remove their jackets'. *Not* their ties though.

Picnicking in the car-park is the grandest of the Season: linen table-cloths, crystal, silver, flowers.

From Caroline's Diary

Our 3rd fraught Open Evening at a school this month. This time, it was Emma's teachers, forcing us to worry years ahead about her chances/subjects for Os, As, even university, to the very crack of doom. Cheap vino and abbreviations like UCCA – saw H brighten, kicked him. The mistresses wearing name badges – H made a thorough study of the bosoms.

Jamie doing his As. They go on so long, and he's so stiff upper, tho feeling grim in secret. H says the telephone bill will be double with all the reversed charges, but he positively leaps for it when it rings, to be first with the shoulder.

Eton boys at Henley; Jamie plays the twit

Old Pangbournians who never grew up. Henley has more zebras than a zoo

THE CANCER SLOANE

June 22nd, enter the Cancer Sloane

The Cancerian Sloane has this calm controlled façade – and underneath a *raging* ferment. But when the shell cracks, everyone just says: 'crabby old bag'.

That doesn't stop them from telling the Crab their troubles. You have a reputation as a sympathetic person – but maybe you're just a good listener. You find it awkward revealing *your* deep feelings – you can't believe anyone really wants to know.

Another side of you is your loony sense of humour – you love Rowan Atkinson and the Python team. When you're in the mood, even a faintly amusing remark can trigger off an uncontrollable fit of giggles.

There's nowhere you'd rather be than in the bosom of your family (though, when it comes to the monsters, that doesn't mean that you don't thank God for boarding-school). Christmas is one of your favourite times, with all your relations in jolly spirits under one roof.

You are house-proud and have a flair for making anywhere feel like home. It's an outlet for your Cancerian creativity, full of sentimental mementoes (*and* junk).

Friends think you're a bit gullible and romantic – too good for this cut-and-thrust world.

Your secret: You wish you'd never had to grow up.

Swig, swig together

Sloanes congregate at the Bridge or Fawley Bars, or the Champagne Lawn. Most people do watch a few races, but you have to drag yourself away from your Pimm's – they mean it when they say 'No glasses beyond this point'.

Thursday is the most concentrated day of racing – one every five minutes. The boats shoot past, pulling their wave of clapping behind them. You follow the Ladies' Plate (university and college

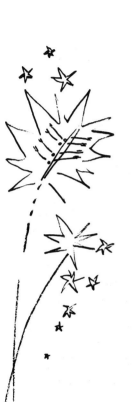

eights) and the Special Race for Schools, run at the weekend to avoid exams. The more prestigious schools race is the Princess Elizabeth, held every day; one year Eton had a police escort to rush them from A-levels to the race.

At the end of a long day you retire to a pub – either the Little Angel or the Horns. In the evening the restaurants in Remenham, Henley and Sonning get jolly boating families on their way home. It is elegant to dine in the Leander Club, but you have to go with a member.

Spot the active rowers at dinner: the men ordering a 'Leander Special' – pint of orange juice and lemonade mixed, with a dash of Angostura bitters.

Other happinesses during Henley are the Leander Club ball (float, float forever, with our partners between our knees) and the fireworks on Saturday night. The place to watch the fireworks is the hill above the river. The local hoi polloi are all there, but never mind. Jolliest summer ever, we gasp, gasp together (concerted 'Oooohs') as the rockets soar up and break over the Thames. Then the young Sloanes whizz off to the fair on the other side of the bridge. Jamie wins two gold fish which he calls Leander and Hellespont and, after a fair wallop of the Octopus and the Roter, Sophie is overcome. She forthwith contributes her £13 investment of strawberries and champagne to the beautification of Henley.

The garden and larder
The green drawing-room

Roses, peonies and larkspur delicious, which look good for the drinks, swims, cricket, croquet, drinks, tennis, dances, drinks, wedding and weekending. The 'conservatory saga' gives one masses to talk about. Henry enjoys his own joke 'Not so much Chatsworth as Chatup-the executors to see what Uncle George is worth.'

The strawberries are coming on – essential to life but 'jolly tasteless these days'. You coax them to be ready for the 4th of June. You crouch over them before Glyndebourne, Ascot, Henley, cricket matches and speech days. (Actually, everyone prefers raspberries –

From Caroline's Diary

Continually making status picnics, getting into irreproachable Dowdy and setting off for a sports day. The girls' schools seem determined to create their own more lavish 4th of June – the battle of the sexes won on the picnic fields of Tudor Hall.

Henry bravely went in for the fathers' race and came 5th. As Emma said loudly, it's always the father with the shortest legs who wins.

HENRY'S
GUIDE TO ASSOCIATE PERFORMANCE APPRAISAL
PERFORMANCE DEGREES

PERFORMANCE FACTORS	FAR EXCEEDS JOB REQUIREMENTS (1)	EXCEEDS JOB REQUIREMENTS (2)	MEETS JOB REQUIREMENTS (3)	NEEDS SOME IMPROVEMENT (4)	DOES NOT MEET MINIMUM REQ. (5)
QUALITY:	Leaps tall buildings with a single bound	Must take running start to leap over tall buildings	Can only leap over a short building or medium with no spires	Crashes into buildings when attempting to jump over them	Cannot recognize buildings at all, much less jump
TIMELINESS:	Is faster than a speeding bullet	Is as fast as a speeding bullet	Not quite so fast as a speeding bullet	Would you believe a slow bullet?	Wounds self with bullets when attempting to shoot gun
INITIATIVE:	Is stronger than a locomotive	Is stronger than a bull elephant	Is stronger than a bull	Shoots the bull	Smells like a bull
ADAPTABILITY:	Walks on water consistently	Walks on water in emergencies	Washes with water	Drinks water	Passes water in emergencies
COMMUNICATION:	Talks with God	Talks with angels	Talks with himself	Argues with himself	Loses those arguments

shorter season, more expensive, from Scotland. But they're only safe in restaurants or chez pernickety Virgo Sloanes – otherwise, grubs.)

You're busy: mowing, picking fruit and vegetables. The greenfly, it appears, like garlic. Suffering from backache from hoeing, mowing, weeding and straw-berrying, you sow more lettuces. You try not to have to stake the border plants: staking is municipal. You plant floppy plants beside sturdy shrubs to do the work for you, ie peonies behind roses.

Caroline collects roses to make her pot-pourri (receipt and ingredients from Culpeper). The airing cupboard smells like Floris but the garden looks as if locusts have stripped it. The Kimbolton-Smiths drop in that day.

Larder and freezer
You pick and pick and pick and pick: things grow better if picked. As soon as you have more than you can eat, you start feeding the freezer. Some Carolines get so carried away they forget to eat things fresh and only go outside at all to get more for the freezer. You know you've become a freezer-slave when you have to take something you've just put in straight out again to have a veg for dinner.

On Henry's mind

• Whether the children will pass.
• The Old Boys' match at Jamie's school, the fathers' race at Edward's school, the sack race at Emma's school (a father fell down dead during it a few years ago). And not being spotted by the office at the Test Match.
• His speech at the wedding.
• Whether he'll be able to recognise the office when he goes back to it.
• Assessing the employees for 1 July rises. The employee has to sign what the boss thinks of him, and this is where it breaks down, since male Sloanes have no moral courage. The females have it all (or is it a bossy punitive streak?).
• But creeps, being ambitious, move on. Henrys ring each other: 'I've got some good news and some bad news – which do you want first?'
'The good news.'
'Martin is leaving us.'
'Congratulations. That's great. What's the bad news?'
'He's coming to you.'

Forward planning

★ Make dentists' appointments before the autumn term.

JULY

Days 16 hr 3 min (av), shortening

* Income tax due, 1st
* Red deer shooting starts, Scotland: stags, 1st
* Princess of Wales's birthday, 1st (b 1961)
* Eton v Harrow cricket match, Lord's, Saturday (Jamie says Harrow got its name because being with such ghastly people is a harrowing experience)
* Royal Agricultural Show, Stoneleigh, Warwickshire, first Mon to Thurs (most horsy societies have an office in Stoneleigh so horsy Sloanes go several times a year)
* American Independence Day, 4th (Sloanes at Preppy parties)
* Royal garden parties at Buckingham Palace, on three successive weeks (unmarried daughters may go with their parents)
* Peterborough Hound Show (Caroline in hat)
* Great Yorkshire Show, Harrogate, Tuesday to Thursday
* Royal Tournament, Earl's Court (dashing soldiers, literally)
* British Open golf championships: club varies, St Andrews decides (golf used to be Sloane before TV, and still is in parts: Muirfield, Royal St George's, President's Putter in January)
* Promenade concerts start at Albert Hall, until September
* Final of Cowdray Park Gold Cup (international polo fans elbow out the loyal ones who came to all the first rounds)
* British Croquet Association open championships, Hurlingham
* British motor racing Grand Prix, Silverstone ('Daddy, why's it pricks?' 'Because it's French.')
* International Polo Tournament, Windsor Great Park (since the Prince of Wales played in it just before his wedding, it's gone 'public')
* Test Matches
* Royal International Horse Show, Wembley, Monday to Saturday
* Royal Welsh Show, Builth Wells
* Schools break up around 19th
* Highland Games start: Inveraray, Tobermory and Inverness are in July
* King George VI and Queen Elizabeth Diamond Stakes, Ascot
* Benson & Hedges cricket cup final, Lord's
* Christie's annual evening reception and preview of next season (if you're a Christie's family)
* Sotheby's ditto (if you're Sotheby's)
* Benson & Hedges European showjumping championships, Hickstead
* Summer sales in the shops (it's always the weather to buy a classic woollie)
* Parliament breaks for summer recess
* Fordingbridge Show, third Saturday (biggest Heavy Horse showing in South of England – the Michael Carpenter Cup)
* The Game Fair, last Friday to Sunday (1984, 27th–29th at Broadlands, Romsey; place varies but Sloanes would follow it anywhere)
* Goodwood, last Tuesday to Saturday

Snow report

A heavy fall of brochures on the mat
Ski brochures for next season are published. Snociable Sloanes are already on most mailing lists, but brochure publication is traditionally announced on the inside back page of *The Times*. Rumours about which company presently has the jolliest/most competent/prettiest chalet girls carry a surprising amount of weight, as do rumours about which company is about to go bust. Rumours of financial instability are part of the air of the Alps, though few can be substantiated.

Whichever company Hooray parties book with, as soon as they are on the piste or in the bars they pretend to be with another, which then gets the blame/bill for their misbehaviour. But the bill of Supertravel punters pretending to be with Bladon Lines roughly equals the bill of Bladon Lines punters pretending to be with Supertravel.

Sloanes in the Mall before going to the Pal. 'Don't preen – I doubt if *you'll* talk to the Queen'

Keen skiers who want a particular chalet book it immediately the brochure comes out. However, these keen beans find it hard to get their friends to commit themselves so far ahead. July evenings sipping Pimm's in the garden of the Windsor Castle should be used for discussing the Game Fair, not next year's skiing holiday.

When Sloanes drop out

Off to another kind of boarding-school

Sloanes are not natural druggies, they prefer to get drunk. Drunkard is a term of approbation for Sloanes. But Sloanes

STRAWBERRIES ROMANOFF

It doesn't matter how often Sloanes are given strawberries and cream, as long as it's during the Official Strawberry Season, which is during June and July. A true Sloane would never eat a strawberry at any other time of year. It would not seem at all right. This pudding varies the theme nicely.
For 3–4

1 lb strawberries ● ½ pint double cream ● the grated rind of 1 orange ● 2 egg whites ● 4 oz caster sugar ● 2 tbsp brandy or curaçao ● 3–4 tbsp crushed ratafias ● angelica to decorate

Hull and halve the berries. Whip the cream with the orange rind and half the sugar. Whisk the egg whites semi-stiff, fold in the rest of the sugar and continue whisking until they form soft peaks. Fold the egg whites into the cream. Add the brandy or curaçao. Reserve a few half strawberries for decoration and fold the rest into the cream.
　　Serve it in large, elegant glasses. Put a tablespoon of the ratafias in the bottom of each glass, spoon in the cream mixture and decorate with strawberries and stalks made of angelica.

Caroline to her father

H, Sophie and I went to the beano at B Pal yesterday. There were thousands of us. The sight of the long queue winding its way up to the door soon puts paid to delusions of grandeur, despite the morning suits!!! I wore my new pink hat – the one H calls the Wreck of the Garden Hose.

Didn't see much of the inside, just a bit of gilt and red carpet before we were ushered on to the terrace. Was dying to have a snoop! The gardens are enormous – you would never believe it from the outside – and absolutely enchanting with a lake, flamingoes and a band playing G & S. We kept on having to hide from colleagues of Henry's – he can never remember their names. I thanked God for the Wreck.

But guess who we did bump into? The Rustleton-Blyths!!!! God knows why he was asked after you-know-what. Anyway a sticky situation was averted by the arrival of HM. H said she looked jolly grumpy. Well, wouldn't you if 6000 people were tramping over your garden and criticising your fuchsias?

Must dash now. Have to pick up Emma from swimming. She's taking her Bronze today in Henry's pyjamas (Jamie and Edward refuse to wear them these days).

Do look after yourself –

Lots of love, Caro xxx

like hanging round the aristocracy, and they sometimes catch something from them – drug-addiction.

Speed is far too streety for Sloanes (jolly hard to get hold of anyway), as is glue-sniffing (very Tesco). Amyl nitrate, once the darling of the schoolboys, is completely out, along with magic mushrooms. If a Sloane will take a drug it will be one that is expensive, ie cocaine or heroin, the so-called champagne drugs. Lavatories in some stockbroking firms are full of cocaine-sniffers and senior partners wondering where all the cloakroom mirrors have disappeared to.

Becoming *addicted* to drugs is not really done. Like homosexuality, anorexia and depression, it's something that happens to other people's families. If it does it is kept very quiet (pas devant les guests) and the word clinic is never mentioned (sounds too much like one of those documentaries on Channel 4).

A year in a drug-clinic costs thousands. Of these clinics, Broadway is reckoned to be one of the most successful. It uses the Minnesota Method, which will rid you of all drug-dependence: and that includes alcohol (think again next time you see a Perrier Sloane). The family has to be prepared to make the long trek to Weston-Super-Mare (where?) every Sunday to take part in a three-hour encounter group. This is why most families choose clinics nearer London (addicts are city-based). Charter Clinic also take their patients off drink, and the Priory demand a £1,000 deposit for those liable to bolt.

Sloane cold-turkey farms

ALPHA HOUSE, Droxford, near Southampton, Hampshire (04897 210)
BOWDEN HOUSE, London Road, Harrow, Middlesex (864 0221)
BROADWAY LODGE, Old Mixon Road, Weston-Super-Mare, Somerset (Bleadon 812319)
CHARTER CLINIC, 1 Radnor Walk, SW3 (351 1272)
PHOENIX HOUSE, 1 Eliot Bank, SE23 (699 1515)
PRIORY, Priory Lane, Roehampton, Surrey (876 8261)

Caroline to Jamie

My dear Jamie

I have now rung you three times and left messages. I have written, to date, three cards with no reply. As the Half ends next week, I'm amazed at your lack of interest in our plans for the holidays. I now enclose a plain slip like they have for deb dances, and hope that you are not too exhausted to fill it in?

I hope that you are still being schooled and have not been hijacked by some American tourist. Don't let this go to your head if that's the case, just let us know we needn't bother with holiday arrangements for you.

1 *Are you, or are you not, crewing for the Lawrences during Cowes? if so,*
2 *do you need overnight accommodation, meals, clothing, transport, or are you living in or on 'it' – whatever 'it' is?*
3 *Are you intending to participate in any of the social life, and do you have a 'lady' hanging around who may need the advantages of question No 2?*

We have no spare tickets, so you must look after yourself if you want to go to any of the parties.

I am both tired and busy, and expect to hear at your earliest convenience or we go ahead without you,

Mum

I like a girl who can hold her drugs

Goodwood
Racing by the sea
Tuesday to Saturday, last week in July

The last bubble of the London Season (except Cowes, 25 miles away across the water). The shadow of cumulus clouds passes over the Duke of Richmond's and the Earl of Chichester's chalk downs above and wheat-fields hundreds of feet below in an advertisement for the South of England and Sussex-by-the-Sea.

It's smart to invite a house-party to a house rented for the week, as advertised in *The Times, Field* and *Country Life* (from £500). But if you're the normal office-drone Sloane you come by car (Midhurst road, difficult to find so reasonably empty) or train (Victoria to Chichester, then taxi). Lots of car-parks if you don't mind walking, but the nearest – the members' – is small and requires March booking.

Henry and Caroline have become members (£15, Goodwood Racecourse, Goodwood, Chichester, Sussex; 0243 774107) and are paying by the day, £16, as they can't come on enough of the fifteen days' racing to make it worth paying £53 for the year. You can join at the gate: but then you can't book anything. But pot luck is actually OK at Goodwood. If you failed to reserve a table (March or April), there's the seafood and pâté bar, or bring a picnic and lug it up Trundle Hill.

You hope to see some of the Richmond/March/Settrington/Gordon-Lennox family, who own the course. They're royal bastards (Charles II), but indefinably non-Sloane: too professional. You know the Stubbses (carefully inspected during the members' cocktail party at Goodwood House the first evening) would feel happier at Château Sloane.

Sloanes wear kit H, *bleached*. Since Edward VII came in straw hat and white duck, the dress for gentlemen has been panama and light – even white – suit. A few grey toppers and morning coats,

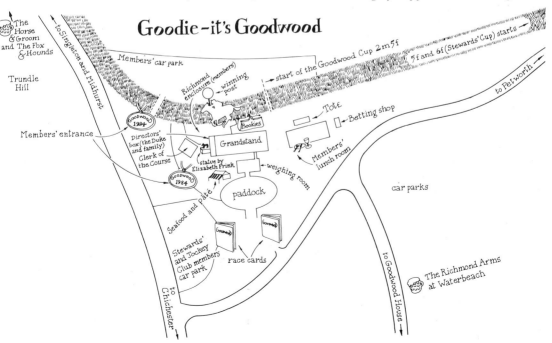

Goodie – it's Goodwood

THE LEO SLOANE

July 23rd, enter the Leo Sloane

Everyone *always* remembers you. You are the celebrity of the Sloane zodiac (or the nearest any Sloane gets to being a star). You have striking looks, you're outspoken – and you're bossy. You have these brilliant ideas – and it's no trouble getting other people, Sloanes or not, to carry them out. They seem really eager (or is it just your imagination?).

People are your thing. You find them *terribly* easy to get on with (and, of course, they find *you* easy). Leo Sloanes love cats – naturally – and children and life, life, life. You are an achiever, an organiser (and a delegator); you're probably branch chairman of a charity or run the local Conservative Association. You simply took over when you moved into the area – no one else had a *clue*. You can't wait to see what's around the corner – nothing daunts you. You can afford to be an optimist because you are the one that makes things happen.

You have bouts of laziness and sentimentality – but generally speaking they're few and far between. Leo Sloanes don't really care all that much about material things – one castle is much like another; as long as it feels like *home*. You're certainly a natural parent – your children have great regard for your good opinion – though they are likely to complain you are always *lecturing* them.

Your secret: The only thing that's missing is someone strong enough to boss *you* around.

Not the grandstand, but the hat-stand at Goodwood

The dreaded French exchange. Hubert, 14, is silent, but we talk *at* him. The obligatory trudge round Bath, Longleat, Windsor, the Hard Rock Café. Emma patronises him madly. Uses his name constantly, either pronouncing it in English or YOU-bear. Can she be attracted? Not sure what present to send back with Edward – H says anything could be misconstrued, and let's give a year's *Private Eye*, le Canard Free-range.

Yesterday we suffered the fête worse than death. But my produce stall made £20 for the church so I feel I can tackle the Vicar about leaving his bats unsprayed and unmolested.

Flying holly leaves???

escaped from Ascot or, Henry says, Broadmoor, circulate insensitively among the business boxes. Henry sometimes wears his cricket club or school blazer and white flannels. Caroline's hat is tethered by hat-pin or elastic – it's Good*windy*, really.

Henry's races are the Stewards' Cup (Tuesday) and the Goodwood Cup (Thursday). The latter is a stamina-test so severe that winner-finding is the easiest in the calendar. And vast though the 6-furlong Stewards' Cup field normally is, Henry knows that – with rare exceptions – the winner is drawn on or near the far rails (high numbers).

But the adrenalin-count at Goodwood is low anyway. No one minds losing here. They go for an unsmart swim on the way back.

The garden and larder
Almost too lush

Petals on the grass. Can't last. Already you are producing the gardener's anguished refrain 'If only you'd been here last week' and looking every morning to see if it has all suddenly gone over.

It is lucky that Sloanes no longer smoke – Monday used to be Caroline's lawn-crawl to pick up fag ends. In her new health mode, she cuts herbs for drying before they flower and hangs them upside down in bunches out of the sun.

Here we go round the parading ring, at Essex Show, at Essex Show, This is the way a Henry rides, all on a Saturday morning

From Caroline's Diary

Found an abandoned baby bat and was having great fun looking after him on meal-worms. He was quite tame – tho H hates him hanging upside down from the curtains! Then DISASTER – he saw jar of meal-worms, climbed in, guzzled all the food and was literally too fat to climb out. An unnerving few hours was had by all until his tum subsided.

The compost has farrowed a litter of marrows for the village flower show. In Mummie's day her exhibits always won and any judge who did not realise this was new.

Larder and freezer

For Caroline it's bottom-up time in the garden and methodical dedication to blanching, bagging, labelling and freezing. Henry says 'You can't get a damn thing to eat in this house – Caroline's always feeding the deep-freeze.' Caroline can't see how she'll get away to the cottage. Henry bolts to Lord's or his county cricket ground. Caroline tries to catch the lettuces before they bolt too.

The fruit goes into ice cream and fools and jelly and jam. 'That thing in the larder is obscene' shouts Henry, after hitting his head on the jelly bag. Caroline goes to bed each night with a bad back and a cup of her own sedative tea, balm and camomile (pour boiling water on half a teaspoonful of each), brooding on job prostration.

On Henry's mind

- The high cost of an 'addict's hotel'. A certain person not a million miles from Henry Sloane has suddenly been detected as being on heroin – after a diamond brooch, silver sugar castor and the Famille Rose disappeared from the Sloane home. (Thank goodness the Mason's Ironstone we *really* like isn't worth much.)
- City joke: *Auditors in the office. Gang breaks in and orders all staff to lie down. All lie face down except Mary. Manager whispers 'No, no, Mary. These are criminals, not the auditors.'*

Forward planning

★ Order Cash's name-tapes.
★ Book place in No 1 Car-park for next year's Royal Ascot (p 70).

AUGUST

Days 14 hr 32½ min (av), shortening

★ Cowes Regatta, first week: Saturday to Sunday
★ Bank holiday in Scotland (1984, 6th; 1985, 5th)
★ Highland Antique Fair, Caledonian Hotel, Inverness, Bank holiday Monday to Wednesday
★ Dublin Horse Show, first Tuesday to Saturday
★ The Queen Mother's birthday, 4th (born 1900)
★ Highland Games: Aboyne, Ballater, Crieff, Oban, Cowal are in August. Cowal is the biggest – serious Scottish games, international competitors
★ Lowther Castle horse-driving trials
★ National 17-goal polo championship, Cirencester Park
★ Grouse-shooting opens (and snipe and ptarmigan) on the Glorious 12th
★ Exam results for O- and A-levels, around 12th
★ Pony Club camp
★ Princess Anne's birthday, 15th (born 1950)

★ Heart Beat Ball, Catterick, Monday of York Race Week
★ York Races, Tuesday to Thursday mid-month
★ Test Matches
★ Edinburgh Military Tattoo, Friday
★ British Driving Society's second official meet, Saturday
★ Edinburgh Festival opens, Sunday, for last two weeks August, first week in September
★ Jumping Derby International, Hickstead
★ Cubbing starts in some hunts (5 am . . .)
★ Argyllshire Gathering, same day and place as the . . .
★ Oban Ball, start of the Scottish Season
★ Sotheby's sale at Gleneagles of sporting pictures and equipment (Henry adores eyeing the guns and fishing tackle and tartaned Americans, even if he doesn't buy)
★ August bank holiday, last Monday (1984, 27th; 1985, 26th)
★ Final of Cowdray Park Challenge Cup

Cowes

Prince Philip speaks only to the Squadron and the Squadron speaks only to God

The Saturday after Goodwood to the following Sunday

The men of the royal family go to Cowes Week. It's more difficult to be 'in' at Cowes than to marry Prince Andrew. It's defended like a naval base for the use of snobs, nobs and bobs (billions of). As the wet joke says, 'Ocean racing is standing in a cold shower in your best suit pushing £5 notes down the plug with your big toe.' Still, it's fun. Even the racing is fun, and you can see it, because the boats start and finish just off the Royal Yacht Squadron steps.

The Island Sailing Club is *the* club during Cowes Week. All sorts taken, provided they are proper sailors. Normally not for SRs, but they have to go there if just visiting because the RYS won't take them, RLYC too expensive and RCYC too open.

Island Sailing Club, High Street, Cowes, Isle of Wight (0983 296621). Temporary membership, £5. You can buy a badge at the door for the week. Then you can use all the club facilities.

Royal Yacht Squadron, The Castle, Cowes (0983 292743). The smartest of the smart. They have sloping lawns which overlook the start, and members sit sipping champagne or tea. Temp membership for owners of the Admiral's Cup and 'Maxi' yachts. Otherwise only members and unlimited guests can enter.

The Squadron traditionally only has members from the professions. Tradesmen are blackballed (each member drops a ball into a box with two compartments, 'for' and 'against'. If there is more than one ball in the 'against' compartment, the proposed is blackballed). There was a member, Lord Henry Denison, who always blackballed when the wind was in the East. But the RYS seems to have lost some of its blackballs. Owen Aisher of Marley Tiles is a member.

Ball on the Monday. A party from the royal yacht. Only members and guests.

The next best club is the *Royal London Yacht Club*, The Parade, Cowes (0983 293153). Any member of the Royal Thames Yacht Club may use the facilities of this club. Crowded cocktail party on Monday ('Prince P. was practically pushed off the balcony'). Ball on Wednesday, members and guests only. All the balls are over-subscribed, and full members have priority. If there are any tickets left, temp members can try.

Royal Corinthian Yacht Club, The Parade, Cowes (0983 293581). Temporary membership badge about £10 for the week. Ball on Tuesday.

There's also the Cowes Corinthian YC, the local professionals' club.

More information from Cowes Week Organisers, Cowes Combined Clubs, 128 High Street, Cowes (0983 295744).

On the Friday, there is a huge fireworks display. Strategic positions are on the Parade in one of the tall buildings or clubs – the RL and RC. The British Admiral's Cup crew often take a flat in Osborne Court and hold riotous parties. The roof and balconies provide brilliant views of the fireworks. A yacht is another good position. During Admiral's Cup year (it is held on odd years, so they are particularly crowded), there is a Naval guardship to the royal yacht *Britannia*, and this ship holds a dinner and dance on the Friday night. Each officer may invite a guest, but there are usually far more men. Mosbies (launches) come to collect people from the steps in front of the RYS and ferry you to the ship – everyone thinks you are a foreign royal cousin. If you don't know a Naval officer to invite you, you can hang around and get chatted up by a midshipman (or the Captain, depending on your wrinklitude). One young Sloane was horrified when a midshipman boasted that he handled a 40-foot pinnace.

Prince Edward at the helm during Cowes Week

From Caroline's Diary

To Scotland to Pa's. There really is nothing like the Inverness sleeper, transport of delight. The most glamorous tweedies on the platform, Willses, Macdonald-Buchanans, lovely yellow dogs (Hannah furioso at their placidity), wonderful leather luggage like a trip to the past. Emma rather interested that she was next door to Lord Torridon, but Henry pointed out that the old all-change-compartments-at-Carlisle is no longer regulation. We walked the dogs at Crewe. Waking up to the fresh moist Scottish air. So super to be here!

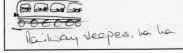

Railway sleepers, ha ha

August

Cricketer at large

The free-floating Sloane

Henry has attended this summer's Test Match (he and other Sloanes keeping KV so as not to be seen by someone from work). Later on, he queues to telephone Caroline to say he's going to be late and strides purposefully if wonkily round the outer perimeter to shake off his lunch (strictly liquid. No pouffy picnics for chaps of the MCC).

Cricketing Sloanes play for a wandering side and like to play in the West Country (the beer's good and lots of friends to descend on). It's the team's August tour. Henry calls it the tiring sword. The Sloane clubs are Free Foresters/Band of Brothers/I Zingari/The Butterflies. The MCC are the least skilful but the heartiest. Wives and girlfriends pack the hamper and the rug and drive the hero to the field of combat in the Volkswagen Golf.

The covering season: people

Me hopeless, you Virgo

1 August to 15 November

You can't make love just when the urge strikes you like a modern person. You've got responsibilities. Sloanes think of themselves as romantic, rabbit-like people, who could have children at any moment. 'Don't give Henry any more to drink!' cry Sloane mothers-of-two when they have had too much themselves. 'He only has to pass me on the *landing* for another horror to be on the way.'

However, there is tremendous planning of these things in the Sloane community. Sloanes used to have babies just before the financial year started on 6 April, to get a rebate. This has now been stopped. But they *like* to do something abandoned in June, a time of aphrodisiacal social gatherings. In some Sloane

'I've got you covered, ha ha. *I'm* the one who wears the trilby'

I Zingari v Eton Ramblers at Robin Leigh-Pemberton's in Kent: padded up and ready to score ht wkt

From Caroline's Diary

Our Cordon Bleu Lucinda arrived to help Maggie. Jamie quite amenable for once to doing the washing up. The Kimbolton-Smiths at the Mains with their 12. Bridge every night, going out in the boat, walking, great feeling of anticipation. Emma and Edward fishing with Macdonald, she caught 3lb trout. Jamie to go stalking as soon as Macdonald can.

Sophie is driving up via York races, with 3 friends. With their Yorkshire hosts they dined with the Halifaxes – H madly envious, v keen to get at their grouse. I would love Sophie to be asked to stay by the Halifaxes with HRH and Diana, but I know it's unlikely!

families, three or four children were all born in March.

Love, lust and logic

But there is a *particular* reason to start children between August and November. They get a summer birthday party; but more important, they are *the right age for school in September*. They *are* all thirteen (thirteen by 1 September for the Michaelmas term), but there are some who are just thirteen and others who are about to be fourteen, and who never get over feeling at a disadvantage as the Old Man or Old Woman of the class. The well-known worriedness of Virgos actually springs from this, not the stars.

Public school is only the worst of the great September watersheds. Even toddlers can't go to school unless they are five by 1 September. It's no good being five on 5 September. You start school at nearly six.

So all along, you have to be as *young* as possible within the age limit. This is the exact opposite of horse-covering (see page 26), where a foal should be as *old* as possible within the age limit.

Henry and Caroline know it's up to them to get Caroline pregnant between August and November. At first, this causes a lot of 'Darling, what fun we're going to have' and 'Shall I get a bottle of the Berry Brothers Beauj from the rack to celebrate your being in season?' Caroline tells her best friend she's come orf the pill.

Doing it with intent starts as a great aphrodisiac (after you have had your three horrors, the uselessness of the activity turns Caroline off it).

Baby blues

Caroline gives Henry mushrooms every night, and on 1 September, oysters and champagne. But October arrives, and Caroline is still having the curse. Even *her* arithmetic can tell her that she now only has one chance left. Just eight days

– seven days – what *is* ovulation? Whatever it is, her mind, from being a gorgeous mountain range of romance and desire, suddenly receives an almost blackboard picture of the situation, based on Biology at Benenden, that television film about one's insides, her gynae and her friends' gossip. She sees the little jelly egg (already called Jamie or Sophie) being caught in the tennis-racket-like fan of the Fallopian tube and making its way down it. Then it pops into the womb with the speed of a pickpocket who's been spotted. There it meets Henry's army of tiny stupid little soldiers. There are thousands of them, but they don't see it. It evades them. They swim around uselessly, bumping into each other. Serenely, like the moon, it travels on and slips out.

Caroline feels she is going bonkers. She buys the special thermometer from the chemist that women use to test for ovulation, which gives your temperature of the day before as well as what it is today. She takes her temperature every morning, as well as vitamin E.

One day, it is two degrees up! She is ovulating. She pleads with Henry to stay at home with a migraine but he says his boss has already said his migraines are spelt G I N.

She feels restless and sexy all day, she's certain she's peaked too soon. Where is Henry??? She rings the office and finds he's left to play squash with Mr Smith-Smythson. He does, every Thursday, but *this* is the bloody limit. She rings the Lansdowne and leaves a message for Mr Sloane to 'come home to his wife immediately, he'll know what it's about'.

For God's sake, does a game of squash take all night? He couldn't have got the message. She rings, he's gone. Two hours pass. He comes in, pissed. She says 'It's *right now*. I can feel it.' He says 'I'm not sure I'm up to it.' She says 'Come *on*. It's going to *drop out*.' He says

August

Jamie jumpy, smoking too much. Then at last the SAE with the A-levels arrived. I was forbidden to open it, could hardly wait until he came in from the hill. But thank the Lord he's passed high enough (B, B, C) to go back to Eton for 7th term and apply to Christ Church.

Whenever Grandpa's back's turned, J on the telephone checking up on his mates. NB leave £20. Some of them are through, some are off to crammers, Will is going into the Army. A parting of the ways for J's little group.

The grouse season

Nice work if you can get it

12 August to 10 December

Grouse-shooting is the only shooting where you like to be there on the first day, the Glorious Twelfth.

The first grouse come rattling down in train or plane and on to plates in the Mirabelle, etc, on 12th. Others come rattling out of the deep freeze. . . .

Grouse are the aristocrats of game-birds, and many Henrys don't aspire to shooting them – too expensive. Every grouse shot costs £20, on a realistic balance-sheet (pheasants: £10). You don't rear grouse, nature does, and only in Scotland, Yorkshire, Northumberland, Derbyshire and North Wales (very

Nissaki's such a larki

'There'll be another one, you know, darling. You're Euston not Oban.' She says 'I think you're DISGUSTING. You don't *care* if Jamie is born on September 16th and is the oldest boy in the whole class, a year behind everyone else *all his life*. Just like his *father*.' He says he'll do his best. Eventually, after a terrible struggle, they flop back in a bed that smells like the Admiral Cod. She just *knows* it won't be any good.

Nightly attempts not to let the egg get away exhaust them. The dread Ovulation casts a gloom over them for a week, then they relax and say 'We've let him down, we've let Jamie down.'

'Or Sophie down.'

'I'd better go back on the pill.'

'Yes, darling. We shouldn't take any chances I suppose. And next year we'll actually be able to *afford* Sophie or Jamie. You do look super tonight.'

'It's probably because you don't have to fancy me until next summer.'

Then comes the frantic search ('I can't *find* it ... it's probably perished anyway'). And a young Sloane is born on 16th September. Half the Sloane population are Virgos, and this is why.

PICNIC EGG & SAUSAGE ROLL

Caroline swears 'there is an advanced form of sausage life in Sainsbury's' (ie they're very good there). The King's Road branch has extra specially good ones (Extra Special Pork) to which Henry is extremely partial. Caroline unskins them and makes a giant sausage roll for the picnics which seem to occur every other day at this time of year, what with the Pony Club dos, horse shows, cricket matches, regattas and other sporting events peculiar to August. She decorates the pastry with horses, bats and balls, name of team, or yachts; or whichever symbol is appropriate to the occasion.

For 8–10

1 large packet of frozen puff pastry ● 2½ lb very good sausages or sausage meat ● 1 large onion, chopped fine ● 1–2 tbsp cooking oil ● 2–3 tbsp fresh chopped herbs ● ½ lb bacon ● salt and pepper ● 6–7 hard boiled eggs ● 1 raw egg to glaze pastry

Preheat the oven to 375°F (gas 5).

Thaw the pastry and roll it out into a large rectangle. Lay it on a sheet of silver foil which will later be used to transfer it to a baking sheet (this movement can be tricky).

Fry the onion in oil until it softens. Snip the bacon into little bits and fry them until crisp. Mash up the sausage meat (having deskinned the sausages) and add the onion, bacon, herbs and a little seasoning. Puddle it about, then lay it like a bed on the pastry, with a wide margin each side and a narrower one each end. Shell the eggs and arrange them in a line down the centre. Fold over the ends and sides to envelope the filling and seal the joins well. Roll it over so that the seam is underneath.

Transfer it in its sling to a greased baking sheet and decorate and glaze. Bake it 30 minutes. It can be eaten hot or cold.

few in Scotland in the last five years, say other landowners happily).

The high heathery country of the grouse moors is beautiful, and you have to walk – even a Range Rover won't save you. This empty country is *for* grouse-shooting. Not much else will live on it. It has its own shooting lodges staffed for the season, and rallies its own army of head keeper, assistant keeper, loaders, beaters and dog handlers, all marching for you, the guns.

Nervously, Henry waits with his fellow guns in the butts with his loader behind him and beaters driving the birds towards them from far away (you can 'walk up' grouse, but you don't get many). Grouse are small, and twist as they fly – hard to hit. You have your pair of guns: 12-bores from Holland & Holland, Purdey, William Powell of Birmingham or William Evans. They are inherited – a Purdey costs £9,500. A pair is needed because if there are a lot of birds your host suggests you all use two guns.

After the drive, the dogs pick up the birds. Real smarties bring their own dog, and landowners perhaps their own loader. Then after a few drives comes the picnic, made by a young Sloane imported from London. The wives may join the guns at this point: lunch brake is spelt differently up here. Most Carolines don't shoot, themselves, but stand quietly with their Henrys.

Once a grouse fell on a wife's head. Thinking she had been shot, she fell down, screamed hysterically and drummed her heels until reassured. A pheasant can break your neck.

Big shot

There is one landowner who does not have paying guns and still does 'big days' – the Queen at Balmoral. A big day

Grouse shoot in the Highlands. Up goes £20, bang goes 7p, down comes £8.50

Charlie to Edward

Nissaki
Aug 12

Writing to you you old sossidge on the day your parents are no doubt voting Tory with their feet, slaughtering those defenceless birds who can't see your father coming a mile off. My Tyrant almost left his body in a foreign land with Byron's, he got so angry with me for using the word f——ing 'in front of your mother'. Face red as his fat tummy, and that's red, I can tell ya. He says our expensive education should have prevented us from the gross ingratitude of using this gutter word, not to mention the parents' kindness in bringing me to Corfu for an extremely expensive holiday.

He usually calls it Cor FU – what can that mean? I think he was cross becos he can't get up on his water skis. Sits on the jetty, boat takes off, Tyrant takes a dip. Ma looks like a liquorice allsort in her striped bathing suit from Littlewoods (oh my God!!). Thank goodness there's 2 loons on the mono skis, brothers from Bedales.

So tara for now, see ya   Chas

August

can have a bag of 500 brace, each man blazing away with two guns.

Not such big shots

All other big landowners. They let their keepers and their shooting, and perhaps themselves, their castle, their snobbery, their butler and their Sloane cooks, to parties of rich Americans and Germans from the 12th for a few weeks, by which time (at around £3,000 a week per gun) they have paid for the whole of the rest of the season's shooting for themselves and their friends.

I bet you're a jolly good shot.

Deer and dear

A party of 20 of you, plus two Sloane cooks, might stretch to taking a shooting lodge on a Scottish estate for a week or two. Hope to get deer-stalking and fishing as well, and possibly golf and social events: a mixter maxter of occupations. But stalking – one man, one beast – is beyond most Sloanes financially, and they don't really like to take the life from those liquid eyes.

Henry moors

Good grouse moors: North Yorkshire. Bolton Abbey, the Devonshires' Yorkshire house, has very good shooting (Stoker 'n' Amanda is the name Henry would love to drop).

There are famous moors at Swinton, Candacraig, Bollyhope, Hunthill, Blubberhouses (100 to 200 brace a day; on others you can walk all day for 20 or 30 birds). Best Scottish counties: Angus, Aberdeenshire, the Borders, Perthshire.

THE VIRGO SLOANE

August 24th, enter the Virgo Sloane

You are a contradiction. You look sensitive; you certainly seem soft and impressionable. But you're not. You do have a terrific *awareness* of life. You understand what's going on around you – you're very perceptive on atmospheres and situations. But somehow you never seem to be able to manipulate situations to your advantage. Personally, you don't give much away. You bear up, you go on and on being wonderful – until suddenly it's Nervousbreakdownsville.

Part of the problem may be you can't stand delegating. But you don't like being bossed around either. You're happiest working for yourself, pottering about at your own speed. You're a self-starter – and only force of circumstance can stop you. For a Sloane, Virgo is quite broad-minded – 'You're certainly not *limited*', friends keep telling you.

You go against the Sloane credo in that you aren't really a 'we' person. You're not family-minded, nor are you madly social. You'd rather be alone, actually.

But you appreciate beauty. Those outright sensations *do* move you – you aren't an intellectual with your head buried in books. You like *real* things – flowers, trees, birds, or a good-looking Sloane of the opposite sex.

Your secret: You sometimes feel that in the Great Game of Life, you got the rule-book with the page missing.

Hoi polloi go to other parts of Scotland, Cumbria, Derbyshire and worst of all, Wales.

Wherever you go, you're still up with the big boys. Grouse-shooting is big business and big business is about the only people who can afford it.

Scottish shooting bodies

BRITISH DEER SOCIETY, Hazelwood, Methven, Perth

BRITISH FIELD SPORTS SOCIETY (SCOTLAND), Glenmore Lodge, Old Edinburgh Road, Moffat, Dumfriesshire

WAGBI FOR SHOOTING AND CONSERVATION, Boquan, Kippen, Stirlingshire

Snow report

Below zero for many chalet girls

Chalet girl interviews begin in London. If you are cooking in a shooting lodge in Ross-shire (far richer man-hunting ground than the Alps), you take two nights and a day off and travel south by sleeper. You have already been screened by a questionnaire sent in with the application form. Typical questions are 'Give fifteen different ways of cooking potatoes' and 'How would you garnish the following?' (chopped parsley – chopped parsley – chopped parsley is the answer, being the only garnish available in ski resorts). Undesirables from catering colleges rule themselves out by putting Grapefruit Cocktail and Mixed Grill.

The interviews themselves are relaxed and polite, but the interviewer must satisfy herself/himself on two points: that you are U but adaptable (you will meet *some* punters who think you're a creature called a shally girl) and that you are neither a nymphomaniac nor frigid (every male punter will retest you on this point).

The decisive questions are about ways of cooking chicken (Supreme, Kiev, Chasseur, yes; but you must rattle off at least seven more) and the amount of food needed to feed X number of guests.

There are also a few jobs for young Sloane Ranger men as plongeurs (dish-washers) in the big chalets.

The garden and larder

Wrinkly

It's gone over, dried-out looking. After the wisteria and lavender finish flowering, you cut them back. Clip all box and yew and Tarpen hedges for the winter.

You pick the first of the Coxes, delicious when not quite ripe, and beat the birds and wasps to the plums. You try to hoe the border but it's concrete.

The lawn is covered with rabbits and molehills in the early morning and Henry keeps his gun on the window-sill. You start taking cuttings for the greenhouse – softwood first (tender sappy things like pansies and geraniums – though many Sloanes scorn these) and hardwood later (bark).

Larder and freezer

The speed at which young runner beans become 9-inch marathon-runner beans leaves you panting. It's also time for the annual glut of blackcurrants. Nevertheless, Caroline manages to get away with the children and Henry is left alone with his rival.

He reads: MONDAY – shepherd's pie. TUESDAY – Irish stew. WED – lasagne. THURS – I'm tired of all this cooking. Do you realise I'm cooking in the cottage at this very moment? Please make yourself scrambled eggs tonight. Darling? XXX. FRI – you are going to the Plunkett-Brownes for the weekend, lucky you. Or you say you are anyway, sly dog??? MONDAY – noodles. Solly. Still feeling Cordon Bolshie. TUESDAY – macaroni. Ran out of moni. PS: BE CAREFUL TO LEAVE THE FREEZER TIDY, NOT LIKE LAST TIME.

On Henry's mind

● Looking up his old friends (hmmmm . . .) while he's at the club and Caroline's away with the children.

● A Frenchman goes to Scotland to shoot grouse and after the first drive is asked what his score is. 'Of those little brown birds that fly so fast – none. Of those moutons sauvages – three.'

Forward planning

★ Ask the fishermen to get us some lobster.

SEPTEMBER

Days 12 hr 48 min (av), shortening

* Partridge shooting opens, 1st (and woodcock, Scotland)
* Duck and goose shooting opens, 1st
* 1st: date on which public-school pupils must be 13 to get in right school year
* Royal Highland gathering, Braemar (royal family, but v commercial otherwise)
* Pony Clubs jumping championships, Hickstead
* Scottish balls (see Scottish season, p 96)
* Lochaber gathering, Saturday
* Burghley horse trials, Thursday to Sunday
* Doncaster races, Wednesday to Saturday. St Leger Saturday
* Last night of the proms, Royal Albert Hall
* Back to school around 12th
* Dancing classes, exercise classes: term starts
* Sell the pony (owner got poor O results or is in second year of As)
* Social Democratic Party Conference

* Liberal Party Conference
* Perth Races
* Northern Meeting
* Ayr Races, the Western Meeting, Wednesday to Saturday. Gold Cup, Friday
* Newbury, Friday and Saturday. Mill Reef Stakes Saturday
* Galway Oyster Festival, Thursday to Saturday mid-month (the O'Sloanes enjoy it. Great Southern Hotel, Galway; Galway 64041)
* National Horse-drawn Carriage Championships, Windsor, Friday to Sunday
* The vintage in France, if a good summer (otherwise October)
* Harvest Festival
* Autumn equinox, 23rd (equinoctial gales)
* End of the polo season
* Fill in UCCA forms for university application
* Michaelmas Day, 29th
* Newmarket last Wednesday to Saturday. Cheveley Park Stakes, Wednesday; Middle Park Stakes, Thursday

The City year

Wankers' banquets

The City is actually dozens of different institutions, many of which have only physical proximity and pin-stripes in common. The merchant banks, brokers, Lloyd's and the exchanges – London Metal Exchange, Baltic Exchange, Royal Exchange and Stock Exchange – are all completely separate entities.

The place bristles with guilds whose tradesmen's names have nothing to do with what actually happens. The Mercers – the richest and the grandest of the 93 livery companies – don't merce any more, and the Grocers don't groce.

Henry can quote the statistics: 28,000 people work in the City and turnover is £15 billion a day.

The point about the City year is the *brass*, the top brass of politics and big money (Mrs Thatcher likes the City and quite a bit of it is like her). Roy Jenkins,

Morgan Grenfell himself, is often at City banquets.

The City centres on boring *banquets*. Bankers love banquets. The Mansion House is always having them and so are the livery companies – and some of them have *wonderful* halls chock-full of silver. What *these* events lack, of course, is smart young people and beautiful women. Lots of City events do have New City people. The New City is sharp and ferret-faced and very unSloane.

So the City gives you terrific places, boring food and a crack at the boring people who matter. But, more and more, it's work.

There are no magic dates when the City year can be said to begin or end, but the election of a new Lord Mayor at least gets the round of banquets off to a fresh start.

September
ELECTION OF LORD MAYOR. The livery company

Doesn't this stuffi go well with one's shirt.

members vote with cries of 'Aye' and 'Not yet,' since the office goes to the most senior of (usually) three candidates. The losers will stand again.

IMF INTERNATIONAL CONFERENCE. All the top bankers (the ones described in Anthony Sampson's *The Money Lenders*). Past venues include Paris, Dubrovnic and Mexico City. Henry would like to say he'd been, but chances are he won't get the chance.

October

LORD MAYOR'S DINNER FOR THE BANKERS. In Mansion House, like all the Lord Mayor's banquets.

LONDON METAL EXCHANGE DINNER. For 1500 to 2000 in Grosvenor House Hotel.

November

LORD MAYOR'S SHOW, followed by dinner which includes traditional speech from the Prime Minister.

December

BUSINESSMAN OF THE YEAR LUNCH at the Hilton. *Some* City people go.

January

LENDING HOUSES' ASSOCIATION ANNUAL DINNER. Roy Jenkins is a past speaker.

Lord Mayor's Banquet at Guildhall. Platitudes make the best sauce

February

OVERSEAS BANKERS' CLUB ANNUAL DINNER at Guildhall. 700 members, including the heads of all the top foreign banks, jet over specially.

March

DRAPERS' SOCIETY DINNER for the Lord Mayor and Sheriffs. The Drapers are the third richest livery company. (The Grocers are the second richest.)

April

LORD MAYOR'S EASTER BANQUET. Dinner for Diplomatic Corps. International Insurance Institute ski races, Courchevel.

May

CITY LIVERY CLUB LUNCH for the Lord Mayor. The club's members must belong to one of the livery companies.

INSEAD BUSINESS SCHOOL ANNUAL BALL, Fontainebleau. The school is the European equivalent of Harvard Business School. The ball attracts business leaders from around the world.

EQUIPMENT LEASING ASSOCIATION DINNER. The association's members account for 12 per cent of UK capital investment.

GROCERS' COMPANY DINNER for Court and guests. Guests are people like the Governor of the Tower of London and the Admiral President of the Royal Naval College.

Sell in May and go away....

June

... but they don't.

LORD MAYOR'S BANQUET FOR THE JUDICIARY. This is biennial, alternating with the banquet for the Bishops. (The bishops are more fun....)

ELECTION OF THE SHERIFFS. The two Sheriffs are elected by all members of the livery companies by a show of hands (no secret ballots here!). One will go on to become Lord Mayor.

STOCK EXCHANGE ANNUAL DINNER.

LONDON CHAMBER OF COMMERCE ANNUAL LUNCH.

LLOYD'S ANNUAL BANQUET.

July

DRAPERS' COMPANY ELECTION DINNER. Guests include the chiefs of the Defence Staff.

LORD MAYOR'S MIDSUMMER BANQUET. For PR reasons a prize is presented 'for contributions to the Arts'. Winners have included Jacqueline Dupré and Michael Tippett. (The City's favourite artists are Russell Flint and Alfred Munnings – *still*.)

July/August

CITY FESTIVAL. School holidays and nostalgie de Brie send Sloane families off to Brittany, Dordogne and Tuscany. The remaining City gents are forced to abandon their usual watering holes and take to the back streets, hiding from the tourists and the City festival.

The Scottish season
Highland fling of Misses Sloane

Walter Scottism and great new nine-teenth-century money made the autumn season in the Highlands popular, following the example of tartan-mad Queen Victoria. The royal family have maintained their visits to Balmoral ever since. The season is an eight-ball marathon.

This is the real thing, not like England where anyone can wangle tickets. You have to be invited before you can buy one. All the Scots there know all the others, and most seem to be related or at least connected by marriage. In 1800, the population of Scotland was one million and there were at least 10,000 noble families. Reckoning on at least four members each, this is 40,000 aristocrats.

Three generations later it is probably 120,000. The titles are ancient and outsiders don't understand them. A young Australian, after meeting the Cameron of Lochiel, thought that Boat of Garten and Mull of Kintyre must be clan chiefs too. There aren't many surnames so the *smart* McSloanes are followed by their estate and preceded by The.

English visitors do not have to wear tartan sashes (who'd dare?), but they have to learn to reel. Lots of young southern SRs have dinner parties to practice reeling before the London season. There are practices in the colder months (too hot in summer) at Wandsworth Town Hall on the first Thursday of the month, run by Harry Verney (405 1197). He has produced two records/tapes of St Andrew's Ball music and a long-running party tape. These and written instructions of reeling steps are available from him at Wandsworth. There is also a practice at the Lansdowne Club (629 7200) once a month run by Anthony Withers.

Girls who have not taken precautions are seen on the train with *The Swinging Sporran* by Andrew Campbell and Roddy Martine, swinging editor of the *Scottish Field*, or the tiny green *Scottish Country Dances in Diagrams*, £1.50 from J. B. Elsley, 60 Lache Lane, Chester.

Pitlochry Highland Games is not the biggest one

From Caroline's Diary

Cubbing with Em and Ed. Early-smelling mornings with the damp air rising as over-dressed children on over-fat ponies canter about uncontrollably to deliver not quite understood messages to the second huntsman. All home exhausted by 11.

This spongy air has covered the paddock in mushrooms and puff-balls, but the worms seem to get to them before I can.

House-party hosts coach their English guests before setting Forth. The male earring gives many young kilted Scots a slightly Steenie look (the Duke of Buckingham, James I's, ahem, favourite).

It's Highland dress or white tie only. Just recently dinner jackets have crept in, but although tolerated they are likely to be challenged. This isn't Chelsea.

There are 'flatties' between reels, but the respite is brief. A discotheque has only recently appeared at the Perth Ball. You're expected to know the Eightsome, Foursome, Duke of Perth, Gay Gordons, Hamilton House, Reel of the 51st Division and Dashing White Sergeant. You must be able to do teapots, the pas de bas, casting off and figures of eight. This is a *sport*, which is taken very seriously – like, say, rugger. The origins of these formal rituals go back to Druid fertility rites. The men yelp like hound puppies and chuck the women about like sacks of potatoes. The Scottish dances are very virile and bare-kneed. In the flatties, it is considered bad form to move one's sporran to the side so as not to appear to be nudging one's partner.

Everyone in Scotland lives in the big hoose, built, crenellated and turreted either in 1450, 1760, 1870 or 1911. One cannot live in a modest 'gentleman's house' in the country in Scotland – there aren't any. There are no modest gentlemen. The land is poor so everyone has thousands of acres.

Decor and good taste die up there in the thin air. Outsiders are shocked and fascinated by the brown, orange and yellow lampshade circa 1953 in their hideously uncomfortable bedroom in the unheated part of the castle. When you run a bath the water's brown and the ornamental fountain on the front lawn empties. Dew settles on the bedclothes before dawn.

You eat like a waste-disposal system – gamy food like venison, grouse and

The Highland Ball in Edinburgh keeps the sporran swinging

black cock, accompanied by mounds of mashed potatoes. All good plain cooking prepared by Mrs MacRae from the lodge. You drive hundreds of miles to balls in dusty, unprepossessing community halls where you meet all your friends, exchange notes on how you've survived the day, and reel frenziedly until sunrise. Surprisingly, alcohol-consumption is minimal. All the daytime fresh air and night-time excess entices you towards gallons of soft drink. It makes you sweat. The old way was to disappear halfway through the evening to change into a fresh shirt. Now you just change partners.

The English are peering to see what people wear under their kilts. The Edinburgh Sloanes already know. They are called Charlotte Rangers – partly because of Charlotte Square where *all* the eligible young males work and partly because all the eligible girls are called Charlotte. The archetype is Charlotte Black. Charlotte Rangers share flats in Dean Village, the New Town and the

AUTUMN
★ ★ ★ ★ ★ ★ ★
PUDDING

Towards the end of the children's summer holidays, Caroline and Labby long for solitude. Country-based Sloanes can slip off up the lane or into the woods with the excuse that they're going to pick blackberries. This is also a good occupation while you're waiting for horse or boat-borne children to come back to the appointed rendezvous. (Caroline is always punctual; the children aren't.) A small basketful of blackberries, elderberries and crab-apples can be made into a delicious version of summer pudding. There is a theory that if you make it in a loaf tin, rather than a pudding basin, you get a larger fruit-to-bread ratio.

For 6

8 oz elderberries ● 8 oz blackberries ● 8 oz sugar ● 1½ lb crab or windfall apples ● stale bread, white or brown, cut into thinnish slices

Remove stems from the berries. Put them with half the sugar in a heat-proof bowl in the oven to heat through and give up a little of their juice. Roughly

cut the apples and stew them with ¼ pint water until they can be made into a purée (use a sieve). Sweeten it with the rest of the sugar, adding more if you like.

Reserve some of the juice from the berries for a sauce, then mix the berries with the purée to make a firmish mixture. Line a pudding basin or loaf tin with the slices of bread, making sure there are no gaps. Fill it with the fruit. Cover the top with more close-fitting slices, and weight it down. Leave the pudding overnight.

Next day it should be stained a beautiful purple, and firm enough to turn out. Serve it with thick, fresh cream, and the reserved juice.

right end of Leith Walk (the only grown-ups who live in Edinburgh nowadays are either lawyers or traffic wardens or social workers).

The eight balls of fire

The Oban Ball is held after the Argyllshire Gathering, which started in revivalist 1871. During the day, men strut about in kilts and plaid carrying cromachs, and sometimes get drawn into a tug-of-war. Women congregate in the Members' Enclosure in point-to-point kit A, from which drab disguise they emerge in the evening, full-skirted, tartan-sashed and often astonishingly jewelled. Parties come over from Mull. The Princess of Wales's mother goes, and the names of people in house-parties are published in the local press. Rowdiness is out. Music: Hi-Level band.

The Skye Balls. These two days and nights, Thursday and Friday in early September, could stand for the whole Scottish season. Somebody once compared Skye with a one-month activity holiday in the Urals. It's run from Nairn on the east coast by Rhuaridgh Hilleary. You come over the sea by yacht or ferry and you're cut off from the reality of the mainland. Gatecrashers don't survive. During the day, you picnic by the sea and get wet. At night you congregate in Portree in a hall bedecked with tartan rugs and clumps of heather. The local people have mixed feelings about this particular influx of noisy society. Some

Wrinklies get roped in to the Scottish Season

years ago, a few radicals threw tomatoes, but the bread-rolls-classes are pretty impervious to this treatment.

Some stylish people use their yachts as house-boats and the girls wear yellow wellies under their long dresses and oilskins. Music: New Cavendish dance band.

The Lochaber Ball. Saturday night on the mainland. Music: New Cavendish dance band. Show-offs with fast cars go both to this, on the west coast, and on the same night the . . . *Aboyne Ball*, on the east coast. The Earl and Countess of Aboyne are there, with masses of Forbeses, etc. The bands who play at these events have become legendary: Most remarkable must be the New Cavendish dance band led by Andy Bathgate, a largely elderly troop of talented musicians, some of whom played in the Thirties with the fabled Tim Wright and his successor, Jimmy McIntosh. For genera-

tions they have performed for two consecutive nights on Skye, and then turned up fresh as Loch Fyne kippers at Lochaber.

Donside Ball. At Inverurie. The Gordon Highlanders go.

The Northern Meeting. At Inverness. Music: New Cavendish dance band.

Angus Private Subscription Dance. Forfar. Tartan and tiaras. Chief Sloane is Robert Steuart Fothringhame in matching Victorian kit. Music: New Cavendish.

Perth Hunt Ball. The smartest of the Scottish balls, always tartan and always jewels. Held at the City Hall. Faint smell of moth-balls. Every Sloane seems to come to the races – the punters are better than the performers. Music at the ball: New Cavendish again.

Key London reeling events
REEL AFFAIR Ball, Feb (Michael Marcel, 352 8615)

FOOLISH HOOLEY, March (Anthony Withers, 937 2077)

HIGHLAND Ball, March (Maurice Robson, 251 1644)

ROYAL CALEDONIAN Ball, May (602 6074)

LANSDOWNE CLUB SUMMER Ball, June (629 7200)

MUCKLE FLUGGA, Oct (Andrew Colville, 588 4545)

ST ANDREW's Ball, Nov (Harry Verney, 405 1197)

Countdown to school

Nine days that shake one's world
Day 9, Monday. Are we sure we are doing the right thing? The doubts that have been nibbling the parents all holidays suddenly bite. *Is* the child dyslexic? (the great middle-class excuse). British Dyslexia Association, 4 Hobart Place, London SW1; or the Dyslexia Institute, Gresham Road, Staines, and Bath, Birmingham, Harrogate etc.

Should he/she be going to this particular school? Now's the time to decide about the spring term. ISIS, the Independent Schools Information Service, have schools listed by area: 56 Buckingham Gate, London SW1 (630 8793). Educational psychologists' telephones never stop ringing in the first fortnight of September. Some ed shrinks: GABBITAS & THRING (734 0161). Panel of 12 on books, mostly London, also Bath, Reading, Oxford.

THE LIBRA SLOANE

September 23rd, enter the Libra Sloane

Libran Sloanes are rare. Most Sloane parents lose interest after their frenzied attempts to conceive in season (p 88). The Libran Sloane face is well-balanced. Not beautiful, but pleasing; a ready canvas on which the rest of Sloanedom project their fantasies (and these repressed products of public school can have some pretty wild ones).

Actually, though, you are not mad on physical contact. You don't really understand passion and intensity; you'd rather have a good book – a biography or something else in hardback. The Libran Sloane is not even that close to the family, though you're *fond* of them, of course.

But you have *heaps* of friends. The house is always bursting. No one that you can really *talk* to, heart-to-heart – but then, who wants to? You like logical discussion, good-natured debate – you can see everyone's point of view. That's why you're always being asked to be chairman of something or other – and because you're a good speaker.

You *are* a bit of a drinker (you call it being interested in wine). You just adore the taste. And it goes so well with jolly Sunday lunch-party conversation (nothing heavy). But you don't just flake out afterwards – you like a good walk with the dogs. Hip-flasks and point-to-points are your recipe for fun.

You are the Sloane who most dislikes extremes. You cannot tolerate people who cannot tolerate things.

Your secret: You don't believe in secrets.

or
BEVÉ HORNSBY (730 7928).
MRS NEWSOM DAVIS (289 0618).
JAMES STEVENSON (631 1209).
TRUMAN & KNIGHTLEY (727 1242). Two or three.

Day 8, Tuesday. Organise photographs. You want the children done, or they want their pets.

Day 7, Wednesday. Try school clothes or buy them. Shopping spree to Billings & Edmonds/Peter Jones/Harrods. Mend, let down, name-tape.

Day 6, Thursday. Appointment with an expert adviser: see day 9.

Day 5, Friday. Dentist appointment.

Day 4, Saturday. Get out trunk, if boarding. Favourite food.

Day 3, Sunday. FF.

Day 2, Monday. Fix school run, if day school. Caroline arranges a Caro/Lucinda/Serena/Miranda ferry service. Haircut – Harrods or own hairdresser. Shoes – Peter Jones.

Day 1, Tuesday. Stationery and fun. W. H. Smith, Tiger Tiger, The Tree House, Harrods, Hamleys or Harry Pinker's toy and stationery depts (loved by girls). Tuck for boarders ('Even Ashdown have relaxed the rule about no sweets now'). Batteries checked for torch, computer toys, watch, radio/cassette. Finish packing trunk. Last FF – Swiss steak.

Day 0, Wednesday. Hearty breakfast. Back to school.

From Caroline's Diary

Housemaster's wife (a real sweetie*) rang (I try not to, it looks so wet), to say Edward's settled in very well at Milton Abbey.*

Edward Edward
Ed, Ed Edward

The garden and larder
Crumbly

The swallows gather and leave. The garden has a dismal purple about it, but after a heavy dew, the yew hedges look spectacular wrapped in glittering cobwebs.

Only a few damsons this year. Caroline begins a batch of damson gin: the trouble is, it takes six months to make and one point-to-point to drink.

Take more cuttings, and bring parsley too into the conservatory or greenhouse. Prune the blackcurrants, cut down the asparagus. Caroline orders some more roses and shrubs to plant in October. Sloanes are keen on the 'winter garden', but not for the drive. It's frightfully non-U to be greeted by splashes of colour. Neither do Sloanes have tarmac drives or house names (if they do they are discreet and not on sawn-through logs). The winter garden is:

Hamaelis mollis, Mahonia bealei, Prunus snobitella autumnalis, white and pink, Viburnum bodnantense Dawn, Daphne mezereum, pink and alba, Cornus schrica Westonbirt, Iris stylosa (flowers Nov to March inclusive), crocuses, snowdrops, aconites.

The children go back to school. Up with the croquet hoops. Into bowls with the hyacinth bulbs for them to give as Christmas presents. Henry mows the rough grass in the orchard for the last time. It's wet and the mower keeps getting choked and stalling.

Larder and freezer

The salmon Henry caught in Scotland this month returns to base and the deep-freeze, including some you had smoked locally (over oak leaves, of course).

It's blackberry time. Henry loves blackberry and apple pie, but Caroline worries about roadside bushes – they may have been sprayed. Makes damson jam and plum jam. Pulps imperfect peaches and nectarines from the greenhouse to freeze: 'We'll have Bellinis on Christmas day.'

But the big task is making the dreaded grn. tom. chut., as the label calls it, with all the tomatoes that haven't ripened. Sloanes keep adding to the huge Sloane green tomato chutney mountain which they try desperately to give away to each other, bazaars and mothers-in-law.

On Henry's mind

• School fees, swollen by Edward going to public school. But he is spared the usual September addition to the payroll, a new au pair.
• Baghdad Jones, so called because he shot his father and entered him in the game-book.

Planning ahead

★ Book sailing course for next summer for the children (Island Sailing Club, Salcombe 3481).
★ Book January/February holiday for the grown-ups (skiing or other; brochures arriving).

'Thumb out, Johnny, and *don't* whine, Emily. I've *got* your winter uniforms now — you can wear them on Monday'

OCTOBER

Charity begins at home

But it never stays there

Start of the Funfam season

Sloanes, being basically unconfident (and a *bit* unselfish), like to say they are doing things *for* some cause. You wear evening dress to pick a slip of paper out of a box; it may win you a bottle of champagne you yourself gave, all *for* the starving in India. Charity = dinner-jacket. 'My charity' is the core of the social round. The Reds say the system's disgusting, but it does get the worldly to give, and three-quarters of the money goes on to the cause. It keeps both Sloanes and noovos harmlessly employed.

President of your charity is an HRH, Princess Anne or someone. Under her are the County, or titled London. Arrivistes know it's the way to get on friendly terms with the best people. You have to choose the *right* charity, of course. In East Kent, Mental Health is the one. In North Yorkshire, it's the Wensleydale Heart Foundation (the Heart Beat Ball) . . . But if you've signed up with the dulls, don't despair – you can have two or three charities, or gradually slide over – 'I can't help, alas – I've been roped in by my sister-in-law for her Action for the Crippled Social Climber.' Sloanes are 'roped in' or 'inveigled'. And you give friends *your* list of helpful Sloanes.

'How does one hear about charity balls?' is the constant cry. It's easy, though easi*est* if you're on the committee. The dates are in *Harpers & Queen* in March, in *The Times* etc, but large charity balls are usually held in the same month, the same taffeta and the same place. You can ring up, say, the Banqueting Manager of Grosvenor House, and ask from whom you can get tickets. Or you can ring the charity (p 104).

Country Sloanes object to outsiders trying to get in – the dance is for 300 *of* our friends. When rung up by the butcher's wife, they 'play it by ear' – try to judge how nice she is, and how much help she will be with other charity work. It's only the parties Sloanes like to keep to themselves.

Charity bollocks

Committee of 40 to 50 (only half a dozen do any work), all supposed to bring a party of at least four socially-attractive people with pockets full of crispies for the hidden extras – raffle tickets, tombola, and the truly symbolic writing-your-name-on-a-pound-note-and-giving-it-to-the-person-who-comes-to-your-table.

Patrons, around 12. The ones called Mrs or Esq have worked like slaves and probably given the wine or the flowers or the printing bill. The Marchionesses, Countesses etc are there for their titles.

Royal personage. She or he was asked at least six months ago. Some people say you can't ask another HRH if the first says No, but the real charity pros aren't so diffident. Princess Michael (PMK) is a super trouper, and really gets down to selling the raffle tickets.

Be sure to ask people who can't come, so they'll send donations. Alas, ticket prices, at £20 to £30, have soared above what the average Sloane will send (£5).

Country bollocks make more money than London bollocks – staff cheaper and you borrow the local stately home.

There are famous charity-event organisers, eg jolly Iris Banham-Lee of Mere, Wiltshire (inventor of People and Places and the late Belgrave Beano), and seriously good (seriously!) Pam Weisweiller of Hillsleigh Road, W8 (Jinja, etc).

Season: October to July, though little in Feb (skiing, Barbados) and no use trying to squeeze anything new into June.

Other charity funkshuns

Fashion show
Borrow the stately and get several fashion houses, or a magazine, to organise a show, preferably modelled by young wives and daughters. Fairly money-making, very scene-making.

Charity orchsun
Pay too much for picture or vase or other unwanted things galleries and Sloanes have been inveigled into giving.

Gala performance
Covent Garden etc find themselves dancing or singing for a 99 per cent philistine audience, only about 20 of whom have ever been there for pleasure.

Jumble sale
Preview of the best things at the chairman's house the day before, at which everything good is bought – £1,000 raised. Main work next day is stopping people pinching things: with entrance fee (20 to 30p), another £2,000 raised.

Charity supper
Sloane home-cooking, each doing a dif-

Slaving for the British Racing School at the Royal Ascot Ball

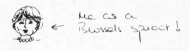

From Caroline's Diary

Rather braced by nip in the air. Am I becoming a Brussels sprout?

Going to Wylye because we can stay with Sarah (tho she'll give me the annual inferiority complex) and also because as H says, the noovos don't. Burghley was as crowded as Oxford Street.

Me as a Brussels sprout! ←

ferent thing. Shaming – people find out who did what before serving themselves. Number of people times price of tickets should be profit (donations should pay for expenses).

Christmas sale

Sloanes man stalls in church halls, end November, beginning of December. Charity Christmas cards, your own cakes, cosmetics cadged from Mary Quant, knitting knitted by nannies.

Conservative Party

Often there's only one club in the village, the Conservative club, so people go who aren't. After you've given your set amount to Central Office you've still got to run the constituency: barbecues, coffee mornings.

Old people's tea-parties

Through the Red Cross or Darby & Joan clubs. Most Sloane helpers are older than the old people they're helping.

Flag day

Have to get permission from police, but it's wonderful fun 'walking the streets'. Dress for church – or wedding. Mustn't look as though *you* need money.

House-to-house collection

You map out a social circuit: Old Rectory (elevenses) to the Manor (teatime).

The Sloane view of charity work

If it didn't exist it would have to be invented.

Sloane bollocks for a good cause

(Not all are registered charities)
B = ball, YB = young ball
(telephone numbers are those of ball organisers)

TO HELP CHILDREN AND TEENAGERS
ACTION RESEARCH FOR THE CRIPPLED CHILD Bs – eg Volkswagen B, Dec (Mere 860136)
FEATHERS CLUBS ASSOCIATION Feathers YB, Dec (723 9167)
GAP ACTIVITY PROJECTS Oyster B, March (Reading 872869)
HOSPITAL FOR SICK CHILDREN GOSH (Great Ormond Street Hospital) B, May (223 5438)
INVALID CHILDREN'S AID ASSOCIATION Black and White B/YB, April; Crystal YB, Dec (730 9891)
JINJA GROUPS TRUST Spring B, May (727 5143)
KIDS Peacock YB for 16–25s, Jan; Carnival in Rio B, June (969 2817)
MALCOLM SARGENT CANCER FUND FOR CHILDREN Bs (940 3224)
NSPCC Cinderella B/YB, Dec; Bluebird YB, Jan (580 8812)
SAVE THE CHILDREN FUND Masquerade YB, July (703 5400)
UNICORN THEATRE FOR CHILDREN Unicorn B, Oct (720 1515)

HORSES
BRITISH RACING SCHOOL Royal Ascot B, June (228 6930)

DOGS
GUIDE DOGS FOR THE BLIND St Andrew's B, Nov (464 1433)

FORCES
ROYAL BRITISH LEGION Poppy B, Oct (581 0999)
STAR AND GARTER HOME (for severely wounded servicemen) Halloween B, 31 Oct (581 0999)

OUR TEAMS
BRITISH SKI FEDERATION B, April (235 8227)
ST MORITZ TOBOGANNING CLUB small Skeleton B or bumper Cresta B, Nov (582 8539)
BRITISH OLYMPIC YACHTING APPEAL B, June (387 3448)

COUNTRY, CONSERVATION, KILLING
BRITISH FIELD SPORTS SOCIETY Hunt Bs via Master of Foxhounds Association (02858 3378). Any profits from the Foolish Hooley, March (937 2077) go to BFSS
COUNTRY LANDOWNERS' ASSOCIATION; SCOTTISH LANDOWNERS' ASSOCIATION have something better than a B – the Game Fair
GAME CONSERVANCY B, May (Fordingbridge 52381)
NATIONAL TRUST Bs (222 9251)

Edward's first bollock: 'Watch out for his teeth scaffolding, Miranda!'

From Caroline's Diary

Parents' committee meeting. Others all MPs/actors/famous/glamorous. H says I've got my speciality too – bossiness. He was at school with 3 of the parents. Planning the bazaar. First log fire of the year, chestnuts and crumpets with Em and Ed. I'm very lucky.

OTHER EXCUSES TO DANCE

ASSOCIATION FOR SPINA BIFIDA AND HYDROCEPHALUS ASBAH (formerly Crown Jewels) B, May (581 0999)
BRITISH EPILEPSY ASSOCIATION Masked B/YB, Nov (499 7674)
BRITISH HEART FOUNDATION Midsummer B, June (381 4724); Heart Beat YB, August
BRITISH RED CROSS SOCIETY Red Cross B (730 0672)
BRITISH SPORTS ASSOCIATION FOR THE DISABLED Mistletoe B, Nov (581 0999)

CITY OF LONDON DYSLEXIA CHARITY Derby Day B, June (581 0999)
CONSERVATIVE PARTY Lots of Bs – including Winter B, Feb and Blue B, June (222 9000)
DISTRESSED GENTLEFOLK'S AID ASSOCIATION Bs (229 9341)
GREATER LONDON FUND FOR THE BLIND Blizzard YB, January; Heatwave YB, July (262 0191)
MENCAP Spring B, May (253 9433)
NATIONAL ASSOCIATION FOR MATERNAL AND CHILD WELFARE Gatsby B, Feb (581 0999)
NATIONAL AUTISTIC SOCIETY Glitter B, Nov (451 3844)
ORDER OF MALTA VOLUNTEERS White Knight B, Dec (730 1653)
QUEEN ALEXANDRA ROSE DAY Rose B/YB, May (748 4824)
QUEEN ELIZABETH'S FOUNDATION FOR THE DISABLED Garden B, June; Metallic YB, Dec (Basingstoke 881367)
ROYAL CALEDONIAN SCHOOLS Royal Caledonian B, May (622 6074)
ROYAL LONDON SOCIETY FOR THE BLIND Limelight B, New Year's Eve (624 8844)
RNLI Lifeboat and Mermaid B, Dec (928 5743)
ST JOHN'S AMBULANCE Order of St John B, Dec (235 5231)
VISION CHARITY Vision B, Nov (768 1211)
Other balls held in aid of different charities each year: Berkeley Square B, July; Mayfair B, Oct; St James's B, March; Sixties B, Oct; Westminster B, June.

FUND-RAISING FOR CHILDREN'S CHARITIES

NSPCC (NATIONAL SOCIETY FOR THE PREVENTION OF CRUELTY TO CHILDREN, 580 8812)
January
Bluebird party at the Hyde Park Hotel, for 3 to 8-year-olds (used to be run by Miss Ballantine before she gave up her dancing classes).
March
Young League party at the Basil Street Hotel. Nannies, organdie frocks, entertainer, 3 to 7-year-olds.

Miranda Laird-Craig opens the competition for the best-turned leg, modelling a blouse from Possum in Chesham in aid of Save the Children

From Caroline's Diary

Ordered invites for the C'mas party and C'mas cards, jolly nice ones done by Molly for the Injured Jockeys. Usual argument with H as to whether it's really OK to print names with the addresses. He says No, but I say some people do it and if he won't, he'll have to do some top-and-bottoming. He can't do the envs after the time they all came back in buff Post Office envelopes.
Went to Jane's bazaar. Felt guilty about having organised cards, bought 100 more for some pink charity. Don't like the charity, don't like the cards, don't need them, don't tell H.

October

Easter
Children's Royal Variety Performance is the NSPCC's biggest annual fund-raising event. On a Sunday evening in a central London theatre, in presence of Princess Margaret (who takes hordes of children). Lots of TV personalities on stage; party clothes. Nanny loves it.
May
Party at Holy Trinity, Brompton, church hall, for 3 to 7-year-olds. An entertainer, a celebrity to give away prizes/raffle wins. Chaotic and noisy, very Sloane, but informal, unlike the Basil Street do.

┌─────────────────────────────┐
From Caroline's Diary

Exercising Polly every day but she's still not fit. Getting self into shape by cutting logs furiously – ou sont les logs d'automne and summer I cut??? Lots of elm, wish it was better on the fire.

   Central heating turned on <u>in parts</u> – blessed hot-pipe smell 2 hours morn and eve.

AGM of Riding for the Disabled at Stoneleigh. All stood in serried ranks trying not to look blue or to catch Pr Anne's eye. Most of us knew her, if conversations to be believed. She watched same old demonstration with avid interest as tho for first time, and knew names of all the horses after 5 mins – Chairman of Group doesn't after 5 years.

└─────────────────────────────┘

SAVE THE CHILDREN FUND (703 5400)
February
Giant jumble sale at Chelsea Town Hall, for two days, mid-February, organised by Lady Hood (Chelsea Branch of SCF).
June and July
Local committees – Stockwell, Fulham, Clapham – all run their own small-scale fund-raising Toddlers' Teas.
December
Christmas carol concert, at the Albert Hall, just before Christmas is always a sell-out. Audience participation (even tinies singing 'Rock Him, rock Him').

ICCA (INVALID CHILDREN'S AID ASSOCIATION, 730 9891)
Three parties every year (this is their new, successful formula).
December
Children's party for children up to 7, at Hurlingham, with entertainer.
Christmas Disco, for 8 to 13-year-olds, also at Hurlingham, in the early evening.
Crystal Ball (see p 18).

Other zones for beaver Sloanes

Amnesty International ● Atlantic Salmon Trust ● Birthright ● Country Gentlemen's Association ● Earl Haig Fund ● Injured Jockeys' Fund ● Multiple Sclerosis Society ● National Art Collections Fund ● NADFAS (National Association of Decorative & Fine Arts Societies) ● Riding for the Disabled ● Royal National Institute for the Blind ● Royal National Institute for the Deaf ● RSPCA ● SSAFA (Soldiers', Sailors' and Airmen's Families Association) ● Spastics Society ● WRVS (Women's Royal Voluntary Service) ● Woodland Trust ● World Wildlife Fund

Beagling

Green coats and gym shoes
October to March
Beagling is the Sloanest hunting, not glamorous or expensive (no Hendon hairdressers, no horses), just running round your local fields after public-school boys in green coats chasing hares. There are 92 packs of beagles, 33 of harriers (between beagles and fox-hounds in size) and 10 of basset-hounds hunting the hare in the British Isles. There are still as many hares. The sport is not 'to control hares'. The point of the sport is the sport – dressing up in your hunt uniform (if you're staff, eg, Aldenham Harriers: canary collar, buttons with AH on them. Evening dress: green, with canary collar and white facings) and running all day in pursuit of an animal you admire. Sloanes think the hare is very clever, in fact magic, and say it grins back at you as it eludes you.

   Hunting Sloanes love the skill they call hunting hounds. (They call one hound half a couple and leave out 'the': 'Took 13½ couple back to kennels.')

cross-country skiing (which the spinster pronounces schiing).

The beagling year

September. Beagle packs go off for a week's training holiday to obscure parts of Wales or the North of England to hunt every day at some unearthly hour of the

A beagling woman warms her cockles before proving she's hard to hounds

UP TO UNIVERSITY

The groves of tinned pâté

Beginning of the academic year. TOTally frantic. You have to find your way round the university / college / faculty / societies / restaurants / pubs, all in a week. You shun the university bookshop and the queues at Heffer's and Blackwell's – Sloanes bring their *A-level* textbooks with them. No expensive course books for Jamie, when he can spend the saving on drink.

It is easy to spot the freshers who have been to boarding-school – they know what to bring. They arrive with teacups, corkscrews, decanters and port glasses, duty-free spirits gathered during the year off, hat/ umbrella stand (with shooting stick, trilby, boater) and a stuffed deer's head. It's the little touches that make a house a Sloane.

Jamie pores over *Hare Hunting* by Lovell Hewett (Lonsdale Library) and *Thoughts on Hunting* by Peter Beckford (J. A. Allen; first published 1781).

Of course, a hunting family's son is sent to one of the five schools with its own beagle pack: Eton, Ampleforth, Marlborough, Radley or Stowe.

For once, Eton does not dominate: Marlborough breeds the most self-assured beaglers. They are the only school pack not to have a terrier huntsman to look after them. Perhaps this is one reason why many of the best Masters of Foxhounds are Old Marlburians (eg Stephen Lambert of the Heythrop, Alistair Jackson of the Grafton). The Marlborough College Beagles do have helpers – an old Sloane Ranger spinster and bachelor (landed gentry) who pull the hound trailer and transport the fields every hunting day, and generally *keep an eye*, as Sloanes say. The man, in his 70s, does it to keep fit for

morning. The Northumberland Beagling Festival (organised by Newcastle Beagles) is the most popular: the Oxford and Cambridge packs are always there. The school packs might be there, or off on their own, with hounds kennelled by the local MFH, possibly because he's an Old Boy. The present boys hope he has daughters, who Jamie and his friends feel need breaking in.

October. Opening meet in mid-October, around noon. Always a lawn meet, Saturday, and often followed by a beagling tea to keep the field until the end.

The field (people following) are half-and-half, Sloanes and locals, with very few noovos (who get on their high horse and go fox-hunting).

Christmas hols. School packs at home again. Jamie goes out with as many different packs as possible, running with foxhounds if necessary. There may be a Pony Club meet, ruined by non-Sloane Pony Club girls making too much noise when hounds are 'drawing' for the hare. Jamie and friends go to the PC dance, though.

Feb–March. Sport starts to deteriorate. Sometimes you hunt 'travelling Jacks' – hares which run long distances. Lambing bars you from some places, but the end of shooting liberates others. Season ends mid-March.

Smart fields to be seen in

(wearing knickerbockers if young). Sophie has even been seen out in scarlet jodhpurs. The 'cap', for the upkeep of the hunt, is £1 to £2. There are hunts with Aldershot, Britannia Royal Naval College, Catterick, Pimpernel (Royal Signals), Purbeck and Bovington army camps; the RAC, Cirencester; Sandhurst, Wye College, and Oxford and Cambridge – the Christ Church and Farley Hill (lots of pretty secretarial

From Jamie's old prep-school friend Anthony

The Joint Masters
The Marlborough College Beagles

request the pleasure of your company
at their

PUPPY SHOW

on Saturday 14th June, 1980, at 3.15 p.m.
at The Kennels, Marlborough College.

Jamie and the old bore join the beagles in the competition for the best-turned leg

Magd Coll, Camb
Mon

Dear Jamie

Lots of Wyks here, but am trying to get to know some new pipples, preferably f. No one at all else in Engineering from a public school. There's a Neville on my staircase who is having an affair (I spose) with another right wallie. Last night they got drunk and competed in imitating Clive James! Etonians don't apply any more – boo snubs to Cam & Ox because they are discriminated against. The barbarians are now colonising Edbrò, St Andrews, Bristol, Sexeter.

I have a nice old bedder, Pam, rather a gossip. Some of the colleges have young bedders who live up to their name. Every year the bedders go on an outing with the Oxford scouts, to the seaside, and Dempster

sends a minion along to bribe stories out of them with crispies! Apparently bedders are a hangover from the homosexual morose Nineties and were supposed to talk to Cambridge men for 15 mins to keep them normal.

Have been invited to join the Pitt Club. Apparently you should, for a year, to be able to eat on tick and go to the Ball. Then you drop out, unless you're the dreaded Pitt Club Type (a Hooray), and all the people from schools which don't get invited rush in and overrun the place. Such snobbishness is the Pitt's (sorry). I must jump into my pit now – beagling tomorrow.

Pip, Pip

Ant

CHOCOLATE CAKE

Henry's birthday is in October (Henry and his friends were born in the good old days; before the tyranny of the Education System necessitated the planning of Human Covering. In *those* days you went into the class that matched your ability). This is his favourite cake. It's also the one Caroline makes best – it's not only foolproof but also totally yummy. The proper chocolate is crucial (Menier's); all good Sloane food shops stock it. Also crucial: a tubed cake-tin, like a Kugelhopf mould (David Mellor has them). Savarin or ring moulds will do, but if you're really pushed, you can use a 9-inch cake-tin with an empty, washed, Labby-food tin in the middle (right way up and weighted down). Caroline fills the hole with a huge white rose for decoration, which saves fiddling about with pretty icing patterns, at which she is *useless*.

For 12

7 fl oz boiling water • 3 oz Menier's chocolate • 6 oz unsalted butter • 1 tsp vanilla *or* 1 tbsp strong black coffee • 14 oz sugar • 2 eggs, separated • 1 tsp bicarbonate of soda • 4 fl oz soured cream • 10 oz plain flour • 1 tsp baking powder
The frosting 2 oz unsalted butter • 4 oz grated Menier chocolate • 4 fl oz double cream • 6 oz icing sugar • 1 tsp vanilla *or* 1 tbsp strong black coffee

Grease and flour a 3½–4 pint capacity cake-tin (see above). Preheat the oven to 350°F (gas 4). Pour boiling water over the chocolate and butter and leave it until both are melted. Stir the vanilla or coffee and sugar into the chocolate. Whisk in the egg yolks. Blend the bicarbonate and sour cream and add them to the mixture. Sift the flour and baking powder together and fold it in. Whisk the egg whites stiff but not dry. Stir a little into the mixture first, then fold the rest in carefully.

Fill the cake tin with the batter. Bake it in the centre of the oven 40–50 minutes, or until done. Turn out when cold.

Make the frosting by combining all the ingredients in a small pan and heating them gently. Do not boil. Let it cool, then spread, or rather pour, it over the cake.

students on the Saturday meet) and the Trinity Foot Beagles.

Not very crashable: the Eton Beagles' visit to the Queen Mother at Royal Lodge each February. There they are cosseted by her lovely grandmotherly kindness, given lunch, then hunt in Windsor Park. Strange – there are boys there one never sees hunting the rest of the season.

Beagle balls with bounce
CHRIST CHURCH AND FARLEY HILL

BEAGLE BALL (Oxford), Bicester, Feb. Precedes the Bullingdon point-to-point and has a similarly wild reputation.
HORSE AND HOUND BALL, Grosvenor House Hotel, London, March. More horses than beagling, but most packs reserve a table. A fine field of Sloane Rangers in hunt evening dress. Splashes of colour, like black – Marlborough – and blue – Beaufort.
PIMPERNEL BEAGLE BALL, Milton Abbey School, March. Renowned buffet – young SR males pile on every kind of cold meat and hide it under a mound of lettuce. Lots of eventing people and Old Marlburians.
JULY BALL, run by Tsa Palmer of Palmer Milburn Beagles fame. (She also runs the Rollerball in April and the Aniseed Ball in January – for the Berks and Bucks Draghounds, held at Elcot Park Hotel near Newbury.)
TRINITY FOOT BEAGLE BALL (Cambridge), Hurlingham, Dec.

The legal year

In with the Inn crowd
Harry, Caroline's nephew, is a baby barrister at Lincoln's Inn. He likes to be seen striding importantly down Chancery Lane in his tabs (*tab*oo – but irresistible), grey striped trousers and black jacket. In the magistrates' court he wears double-breasted suits and a committed frown. He has grown the frown early in life because he knows you rise at the Bar by your gravity rather than your levity. The high point of his day is when at a quarter to six, he tiptoes past the clerks (as disapproving as butlers) with bottles from El Vino's. He nips on to the District Line, back to Fulham, Cynthia and coq au vin.

A round at the bar
Law, like Oxbridge, has a year named after saints and feast-days the rest of the world has forgotten. The Law terms are:
Michaelmas 1st Tues in Oct to 21 Dec

October

The year begins with the Lord Chancellor's breakfast in the Painted Room at the House of Lords after a special service in Westminster Abbey. (Invites to top men only.) Here you partake of small beer (legal ale) and even smaller conversation. In later life, Harry will practise his sycophancy here in front of the judges and eye colleague Arabella (looking frightfully good in black velvet). Sloane women barristers are prone to thick ankles and Renault 5s.

One of the mainstays of legal tradition is Hall. Sloanes love Hall, although they complain bitterly about the food (they dream of the time when they will be sitting at High Table and quaffing vintage port). Hall is the logical extension of Nursery, Public School and Cambridge. Every student has to eat a set number of dinners amongst the Benchers and the old boys who have no homes to go to, before he can become a barrister. There is usually a savoury (anchovy toast, Welsh rarebit) – another anachronism that affirms the Law as the last Victorian bastion.

Towards Christmas each Inn of Court has a Grand Night in Hall. At the end of the meal Harry drinks warmly and proudly to Domus, the house. At Gray's Inn they toast the glorious memory of Elizabeth I in a silver loving-cup full of shandy or something viler.

The Easter Term is heralded by Maundy Thursday. A red-letter day when those to whom the Queen and the Lord Chancellor have been pleased to award the patent of Queen's Counsel (QCs or silks) are announced in *The Times* and *Telegraph*. Harry lays bets in his chambers as to who's Taking It this year. He wins £10 and whisks Arabella to Daly's in Essex Street for lunch. 'Did

THE SCORPIO SLOANE

October 24th, enter the Scorpio Sloane

If Sloanes knew what sex was, you would be a sex object. As it is, people *fancy* you like anything. There is *something* about you. You are strong-willed and straight-talking, and that's an aphrodisiac to other Sloanes. You have fantasies too. A married, faithful Sloane has to channel these towards food – it's the only way to keep on an even keel. (But the old bilges start to bulge.)

You can exhibit the non-Sloane characteristic of ambition. (That's probably sublimation too.) Getting on in life, being rich or powerful has its attractions. You do like a little bit of one-upmanship – it keeps everybody on their toes.

You are devoted to your family – especially the children (chances are they're mostly boys). You don't think you're pushy – you're just right there behind them. They know they'll always have your love and support – the only thing you can't stand is failure.

As for friends, you haven't tons – but the ones you have are there for life. They're loyal to you and you to them. You're seen as a tough judge of character and, you think, something of a wit ('God, I'm funny' one side of your head says as the other comes out with a bon mot).

Your secret: You would dearly like to do something brilliant and arty – but you are terrified of failing.

you see Jones got it? I was against him on the Arche-Ryvell case – absolutely hopeless.' A new silk has to cough up £60 on the nail for the privilege, £120 for the gown.

The Trinity term is when the social life starts to hum with balls and garden parties in the Temple grounds. Wives and girlfriends sip fizzy wine and flirt with flat judges. Harry points out how many people he knows and laughs loudly at the Benchers' jokes. Cynthia cannot get a word in edgeways. This is because Harry has learnt to take the floor

> **From Caroline's Diary**
>
> *Hallowe'en. I took a rowan branch in the car with me, told Emma all Scots do, and we must plant 2 rowans on either side of the gate to ward off evil spirits as at Auchencheyne. We carved turnip lanterns and ducked for apples. Suddenly the village children came – 3 ghosts, 1 cowboy and 1 witch. It turned out they got the idea from ET!!*
>
> ☻☹ 66

(why use a full stop when you can have a semi-colon?);

Also in late June/early July comes the first of the two call dates for the new barristers. These bar birthdays determine your place in the arcane pecking order of chambers. Harry feels very smug: he is three years old today.

After the Gray's Inn Field Club Ball (the most fun), he takes a smouldering farewell of Arabella in the marquee and zooms off to his cricketing tour. No decent barrister would be seen around the Inns in August. Leave that to the criminal hacks (Sloanes keep their establishment fingers clean and practise commercial, tax, Admiralty and planning). In a few years he will learn to take a long stroll through the stone courtyards and lanes so all may see that he's not in Court (ie the High Court, which doesn't sit during August). The Law must be the only profession where to be seen *not* to be busy is the sign of a man much in demand.

The garden and the larder

Putting the garden to bed
Your tasks: clean out the borders while the earth is warm. Plant daffodil and narcissus bulbs outside. Plant trees, hedges, roses, shrubs. Caroline puts in

the azaleas in steady drizzle, gets saturated and sticks the fork through one of her gum boots. A couple of quinces on the japonica exhilarates her.

Henry has his last swim and covers his goose-pimples with his Guernsey and the pool with a blue plastic sheet. On a dry day you make a bonfire of diseased leaves from the roses and fruit-trees. It smells acrid and so British.

Will you/won't you be in next year's 'yellow book'? Every Sloane buys and many figure in *Gardens Open to the Public in England and Wales* or the *Scotland* one, equally yellow, both of which come out in March and go to press in October.

Larder and freezer
Happily, Henry's rival is relatively ignored in October. 'Bring the rats to stay and we'll let them put the apples away on the apple racks' – a PC falls on the mat of a Fulham Sloane mother. You lay the apples out on newspaper in a dry place so they don't touch. They last through to May – even June – if picked after the first frost.

Sloanes eat Bramleys, Granny Smiths and Coxes. Henry says that rotters begin at Calais and French Golden Delicious taste of cardboard.

On Henry's mind

● Livery company's dinner, the Flaxspinners' Company. (Membership purely honorific – Henry spins not neither does he toil. But the annual dinner in ornate City hall reassures one about one's niche in life.) Too much to drink, long boring speeches.
● *What's the difference between a hedgehog and a Range Rover? A hedgehog has the pricks on the outside.*

Forward planning

★ Send for application form for Wimbledon tickets (p 74)

NOVEMBER

* Hunting starts
* Williams Hill November Handicap at Doncaster – end of the Flat
* Guy Fawkes Day ('Remember, remember the 5th of November, gunpowder singeing your bot'). Rams put to ewes
* Christmas bazaars and charity balls
* Common Entrance exams
* Oxbridge exams (Oxbridge entrants have stayed on a term to take them)
* Send Christmas presents and cards by ship (air mail costs money)
* Remembrance Sunday (no Sloane without poppy)

* Prince Charles's birthday, 14th (b 1948)
* Burgundy wine auctions at the Hospices de Beaune for three days (les trois glorieuses)
* Beaujolais nouveau arrives in Britain via fast Hooray, as soon after the 15th as Golf or XR3i can bring it
* Lord Mayor's banquet in Guildhall: the PM speaks
* State Opening of Parliament. Dinner at the Carlton Club the night before: the PM speaks
* Daily Mail Ski Show, Earl's Court
* Hennessy Gold Cup at Newbury – start of the jumping season for Sloanes
* Eton Wall Game (Saturday nearest St Andrew's Day, 30th)
* Tattersall's December Sales at Newmarket

The hunting season
The Sloane hobby-horse
November to March

Going fox-hunting has become much more popular recently. The new rich have rallied to it as a way of getting up there with dukes, princes and Princess Michael. All you need is a lot of money and good legs. What in the Fifties to Seventies seemed a doomed relic of ruling-class savagery (indefensible but irresistible, as Nancy Mitford said) now seems fun, not that cruel, and important to the countryside we all want to preserve. (The blooding of children has been quietly dropped.)

The League Against Cruel Sports, whose sympathisers, the antis (for anti-blood sports) turn up at meets and disrupt them, has done too good a job. They have brought the British Field Sports Society to arms – and there's nothing these old cavalrymen like better. The League won two battles by getting the Labour Party to threaten to ban hunting with hounds and persuading some local Councils to ban hunting on their land. But the BFSS has widened the front by uniting all the other Sloane country sports (shooting, fishing ...) under their banner, emblazoned, oddly but accurately, Conservation. Field sportsmen need the wild places which urbanisation and commercial farming would destroy. And the field sportsmen still have the money to support their sports. The BFSS has recruited the country people, 'locals' in Sloanespeak, to their side. Anyone can see the antis are *townies*. The Society's PRs have successfully polished up the image of country sports ('*Not* blood sports – they are *field* sports').

There are hunts all over the British Isles: 191 packs of foxhounds in England and Wales, 12 in Scotland, 36 in Ireland (and four packs of staghounds in England, two in Ireland). They all have their own 'country' and their history (some date from 1770, many from the 1870s, some from 1970). The bible is the annual *Baily's Hunting Directory* (J. A. Allen). Hunts all have their own special coloured coats, most have special buttons and a different evening dress. There are farmers' packs, there are dukes' packs (the Beaufort, the Percy). There are hunts that meet two days a week and hunts that meet four. The Master is the dominant male in his district, far sexier than the MP. He is styled MFH VC, in that order. The social life that goes with hunting is tremendous – a bit too tremendous when the children are in their Pony Club stage. Can you imagine getting all *that* banned?

There are the dreaded Sloanes who *hunt for fun* and the others, who study 'the mystery of scent' and understand the working of hounds. The dreadeds lollop at the back of the field and coffee-house (chat) while hounds draw a covert. The other type are at the front (though reined in by etiquette – don't overgallop the Master!), pursuing the day's sport and the 'hard women to hounds' – Amazons who are fiercely elegant and always at the right place at the right time. One young SRM met such a girl and all he could do all evening was drool and repeat 'She's hard to hounds'.

Keen hunting Sloanes are usually from a hunting family, or throwbacks (if Henry's mad about it the children may be put off). They prefer a noovoo who's serious to a Sloane who hunts for fun.

Horse is champing at the bit, Henry is champing at the stirrup cup

The hunting accident

So hidebound is hunting that the top hat is still correct dress for gentlemen in many smart hunts, although it has been unsafe since macadam came to roads in the 1830s. Most hunting accidents happen on a road. Colonel Hartigan of the Grafton being killed this way in the 1982–83 season caused some hunts to change to caps, formerly what *farmers* wore. Members of the Quorn now wear *grey* caps, to distinguish them from the Master's black.

But you expect to lose a rider for good occasionally, apart from all the broken necks and backs. Hunting accidents are romantic. You arrive in Casualty on a stretcher in full hunting gear. Your crocked condition is a badge of office – your horse *threw* you – one does not just fall off. A gammy leg, duff arm, broken rib etc must always be due to something Sloane, and noble or mad.

Hunting clothes

Expensive, and in two parts, your cubbing ('ratcatcher') outfit for before 1 November and your smarty Pink (after Mr Pink) or black for the official season. Men – hunting coat (lasts 12 seasons): Huntsman, 11 Savile Row, W1 (the hunt servants are dressed by Bernard Wetherall). Men's breeches: Huntsman etc, or Hebden Cord, mail-order tailor of Hebden Bridge, Yorkshire. Only non-Sloane men wear stretch breeches (all right for women). Boots (25 seasons): Lobb's, 9 St James's Street, or Maxwell, 11 Savile Row. Foxy male Sloanes go to Mr Patey in the Elephant and Castle (1 Amelia Street, SE17) for their top hats – he makes for Herby J and Lock's. The tailor of the black-coated hard women to hounds is Huntsman or Bedford Riding Breeches, 19 New Quebec Street, W1.

Second-hand kits come from advertisements in *Country* (Jamie's Eton clothes came from there too). Or Calcutt's of Sutton Scotney, Hampshire,

November

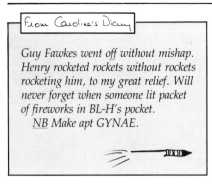

From Caroline's Diary

Guy Fawkes went off without mishap. Henry rocketed rockets without rockets rocketing him, to my great relief. Will never forget when someone lit packet of fireworks in BL-H's pocket.
<u>NB</u> Make apt GYNAE.

can get you most things: a second-hand pair of Lobb's boots for £45 including trees, white buckskin breeches as worn in the Twenties and Thirties – the most comfortable thing in the hunting-field.

Make sure husband/wife, sister/brother give each other white string gloves for Christmas.

The hunting year

August. Cub-hunting early in the morning. Starts late August or early September. Purpose is to rehearse the young hounds, young horses and young foxes in their roles. You hope not to have to sit outside a covert all morning banging your saddle flap with your whip, to turn the young fox back into the covert.

October. Pay hunt subscription before the opening meet (£100 to £1,000. Cap £5 to £40 if you're going out just for the day). Some hunts make it compulsory for members to belong to the BFSS – got to help the Fighting Fund. (But before paying the sub, check that your wife is not having an affair with the Master – a *very* popular sport.)

November. Opening meet, a lawn meet, everyone in full fig. This is traditionally on or after 1 November. But in years with early harvest, can be earlier. Several hunts, including the Quorn and Belvoir, started in the third week of October in 1981–2, when quorn ripened early. As snow later stopped hunting, this was wise.

December–January. Huge fields. Boxing Day meet the best attended. But Master proposes, weather disposes.

February. Around now, many hunts hold their annual fund-raising cabaret – skits unspeakable in aid of the pursuit of the uneatable. The singing at least is bearable (Fred Astaire records, etc). Anything with a top hat.

March. Crops coming up, fox-hunting ends. Fox cubs born April. (Of course we respect their breeding season. We're not trying to *harm* foxes.)

April. The end of stag-hunting on Exmoor. Late March to April the fields are enormous with migrant fox-hunters.

Entertaining Mr Sloane

Dear Mr Sloane,
You say you love me and are looking after my interests. I realise I have your hunting to thank for my continued existence in Britain, chicken-killer as I am. I love slaying. I kill far more than I'm going to eat. We're alike in that. But you seem to have emerged as top dog – I thought you rather unlikely to survive when we two old species were sharing these islands with mammoths, not to mention wolves.

I'm not sorry a carnivore still rules the roost. This new farming type of human provides us both with food, but has recently been annexing my territory. I know you will protect the wild country, because you're a hunter.

I have a nice life. But I would like to make it more thrilling by getting together a group of us to chase you and tear you to pieces.
your fellow Sloane,
Henry Fox

PS: I would pretend it was because you were vermin and had to be controlled – why admit we do it for fun?

HEYTHROP HULLABALOO

This light hearted musical review will be played by friends of the Heythrop and North Cotswold Hunts

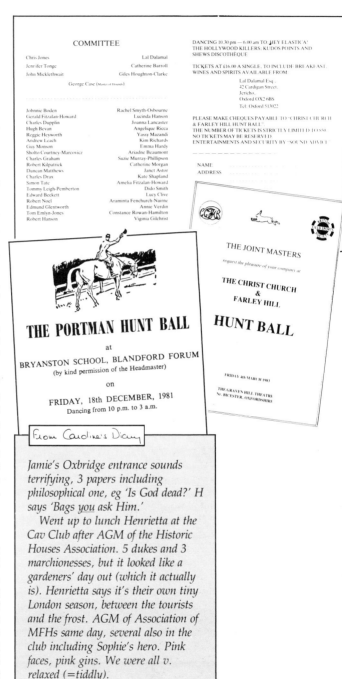

amie Sponge's sporting tour

There are hunts all over the Sloane world: India, Australia, New Zealand, South Africa, Kenya, France, Germany, Holland, Belgium, Italy, Spain, Canada, USA. Jamie in his year off may go in search of hunting. America (as Sloanes call the USA) has 133 packs of foxhounds and they always welcome SRs, eager for the invitation to be reciprocated. Hunting is very good in Maryland, Virginia, Pennsylvania and New Jersey.

Jamie organises a cub-hunting tour of Ireland. He rents a castle through *Country*, hires a hunting SR cook, and invites more hunting SR girls to make up a party with him and his schoolfriends. The girls' mothers only let them come because it was in the CGA magazine. Every morning they get up at 6.30 and every evening they wear black tie. After dinner there is reeling on the battlements. They have hirelings (hired horses). In Ireland, amazing horses appear in decrepit horse-boxes at very short notice.

Out hunting, Sophie is frightened by all those stone walls with big drops beyond, but Jamie copes because he was taught to jump sitting back over his fences. The field is very small – everyone has got special permission from the Master, which can be difficult. Jamie waits on the other side of the fences to look the young girls straight in the eye – his seduction technique.

Hunt balls

The hunt holds its bollock any time in the season or even in the summer. Bad music, wife-swapping, drunkenness, lots of horn-blowing and roll-throwing and showing off on the dance floor (hunting people being ultra-fit). Ends with the Gallop – horn blows tally-ho and all link arms and gallop round and round the room faster and faster and faster. Some fall down. The meet next day is rather subdued.

COMMITTEE

Chris Jones — Lal Dalamal
Jennifer Tonge — Catherine Barrell
John Micklethwait — Giles Houghton-Clarke

George Case (Master of Hounds)

Johnnie Boden — Rachel Smyth-Osbourne
Gerald Fitzalan-Howard — Lucinda Hanson
Charles Dupplin — Joanna Lancaster
Hugh Bevan — Angelique Ricca
Reggie Heyworth — Yassy Mazandi
Andrew Leach — Kim Richards
Guy Monson — Emma Hardy
Sholto Courtney-Marcovicz — Ariadne Beaumont
Charles Graham — Suzie Murray-Phillipson
Robert Kilpatrick — Catherine Morgan
Duncan Matthews — Janet Astor
Charles Drax — Kate Shapland
Simon Tate — Amelia Fitzalan-Howard
Tommy Leigh-Pemberton — Dido Smith
Edward Beckett — Lucy Clive
Robert Noel — Araminta Fenchurch-Nairne
Edmund Glentworth — Annie Verdin
Tom Emlyn-Jones — Constance Rowan-Hamilton
Robert Hanson — Virginia Gilchrist

DANCING 10.30 pm — 6.00 am TO: 'HEY ELASTICA', THE HOLLYWOOD KILLERS, KUDOS POINTS AND SHEWS DISCOTHEQUE

TICKETS AT £16.00 A SINGLE, TO INCLUDE BREAKFAST, WINES AND SPIRITS AVAILABLE FROM:

Lal Dalamal Esq.,
42 Cardigan Street,
Jericho,
Oxford OX2 6BS
Tel: Oxford 513022

PLEASE MAKE CHEQUES PAYABLE TO "CHRIST CHURCH & FARLEY HILL HUNT BALL".
THE NUMBER OF TICKETS IS STRICTLY LIMITED TO 880.
NO TICKETS MAY BE RESERVED.
ENTERTAINMENTS AND SECURITY BY "SOUND ADVICE".

NAME ....
ADDRESS ....

THE PORTMAN HUNT BALL

at

BRYANSTON SCHOOL, BLANDFORD FORUM
(by kind permission of the Headmaster)

on

FRIDAY, 18th DECEMBER, 1981
Dancing from 10 p.m. to 3 a.m.

THE JOINT MASTERS
request the pleasure of your company at

THE CHRIST CHURCH
&
FARLEY HILL

HUNT BALL

FRIDAY 4th MARCH 1983

THE GRAVEN HILL THEATRE
Nr. BICESTER, OXFORDSHIRE

From Caroline's Diary

Jamie's Oxbridge entrance sounds terrifying, 3 papers including philosophical one, eg 'Is God dead?' H says 'Bags you ask Him.'

Went up to lunch Henrietta at the Cav Club after AGM of the Historic Houses Association. 5 dukes and 3 marchionesses, but it looked like a gardeners' day out (which it actually is). Henrietta says it's their own tiny London season, between the tourists and the frost. AGM of Association of MFHs same day, several also in the club including Sophie's hero. Pink faces, pink gins. We were all v. relaxed (=tiddly).

November

The pheasant season
No pheasants for peasants

1 October to 1 February, but Sloanes start in November

Sloanes all shoot, if they don't hunt – how else can you preserve the countryside? (Wish one could do both, like Don 'Four by Two' Fisher – hunted four, shot two days a week.)

Actually, the contryside has shrunk so much that the two camps are in conflict, and on Boxing Day, the hunting Sloanes are chasing up and down the coverts while the shooting Sloanes huddle in their Land-Rover nearby muttering about maniacs mucking up the sport.

Your season starts the month after the official season. 'Only a rotter and a cad would shoot pheasants before the leaf is off the tree,' as Douglas Sutherland says (too difficult?). But, 'when leaves do fall, pheasants be at call.' You can see the buggers, and there's bound to be some shooting for Henry, since there are pheasants everywhere. The average Sloane gets at them four times a year, which doesn't make him a hot shot.

Keepers used to be able to lay on a 'big day', a 'stand still and poop', with 1,200 killed in a day. (The keeper's tip is based on the bag: £5 per day per gun for the first 100 birds, and an additional £2 per 100 shot.) Often a big day would end by killing tame hand-reared ducks driven off the lake. Caroline hated it.

The Duke of Marlborough, for one, still does big days, but the trend for Sloanes is towards the 'small day', the 'rough shoot', the 'walking day'. Three hundred birds in a day is the maximum. Sloanes say any more is vulgar.

Lunch is a picnic, or in the dining-room if near enough. The rest of a North Yorkshire house consists of anterooms to the Shooting-Lunch Dining-Room. Alcohol accompanies or closely follows all shooting meals. At tea, the keeper comes in and announces the bag. For

instance: '384. 150 brace of pheasants, 5 woodcock, 15 brace of partridges, 30 ducks, 10 hares, 4 rabbits, 2 snipe, 2 moorhens, one starling.' The Sloanes laugh and applaud. One shoots whatever comes blundering towards one except foxes, deer or beaters.

Sloanes always give their guests a brace of pheasants and any woodcock they personally have shot. If you get a right and left of woodcock you become a member of the Bols club – and are given a bottle of it.

Shooting Sloanes belong to the Game Conservancy (key man, Richard Van Oss. Prince Charles has taken over the patronage of it from his Pa); the British Association of Shooting and Conservation (formerly WAGBI) (key man, John Marchington, not a Sloane but v. popular with them for his officer-like qualities of organisation), and the British Field Sports Society. The Country Landowners' Association and the Scottish Landowners' Association run the unmissable Game Fair in July, at a different large stately home each year.

Peak

To have your own shooting. Nowadays some private shoots take one or two paying guests to help out. They don't pay as

$\mathcal{D}$evilled $\mathcal{P}$heasant

Henry is shooting every weekend. Caroline is phucking pleasant for a dinner party every week. This is a favourite Sloane sauce for using up the cold remains.

For the meat of one pheasant

½ pint (approx) cream ● 2 tsp anchovy sauce ● 2 tbsp Harvey's sauce ● 2 dstsp Worcestershire sauce ● 2 dstsp mushroom ketchup ● 2 dstsp mango chutney ● salt, pepper, mustard ● dash cayenne pepper

Mix all ingredients together. Lay the pheasant meat, removed from the bone, in a shallow oven-proof dish. Preheat oven to 375°F, gas 5, pour the sauce over the meat and bake for 15–20 minutes, until hot.

much as their true proportion of the total. Eg, ten days' pheasant shooting where the bag is 250 pheasants a day will cost the pg £2,000, £500 less than with a:

Commercial syndicate
Someone takes shooting rights on lease, buys poults from a game farm, hires a keeper to rear them, and about ten guns share all costs. Ten days' shooting will work out at about £2,500 for about 250 birds.

Hooray Henry
He forms a syndicate with nine schoolfriends, sharing costs. They can't afford to rear many birds and so they only bag about 20 a day. Ten days=£200. Very boring for experienced people, but the young men think it's super fun. *Moral*: a bird on the land (£10) is worth two in the butcher's (£5+£5).

The covering season: sheep

Rams put to good ewes
Sheep are terribly Sloane (you share the same taste in clothes). The ram is put in the field with the ewes on or soon after Bonfire Night, 5 November. One ram to forty ewes. Newly-married town Sloanes are amazed that the ram doesn't ruin the plan by finding one ewe he really likes and doing it forty times to her, but ram instinct tells him that every

ewe in the field must bear his brand (a dye harness on his chest). In March all the lambs are born. They're stupid bloody animals – like animated sugar lumps – but you sell the first batch for meat soon.

The garden and larder
Purgatory now or hell later
Everything you haven't done in November you'll have to add on to the spring list of duties.

Caroline buys two small bay trees at £45 each. Henry becomes demented at the bill. Then she goes complEEtlimad and orders three white camellias from Trehane's for pots for the new conservatory. (Tubs must be round not square. Haddon ware is very non-Sloane. So is white-painted garden furniture, especially if it's metal.)

Later in month, you beat the cold by pruning the orchard and cutting the mixed hedge. It's now or February, and it's *murder* in February. Digging done by Jack. He reeks of the tea, beer, even whisky, needed to keep him going.

BEAUJOLAIS NOUVEAU
The first of the summer wine
Any time from the 15th on
It's *always* 'really good this year' (nobody can remember what it was like before). Sloanes have learned to have their Nouveau chilled. They have also *heard* of Côte de Rhône Nouveau (but they don't drink it). Everyone knows someone who's Done The Race to bring the new vintage back from Burgundy (saatch fun – reminds them of *Those Magnificent Men in Their Flying Machines*). After a fortnight of the stuff, it disappears from the dinner table. Livers have demanded decent claret again – even Valpolicella. Also the nouveauty has worn off. . . .

Larder and freezer
'Stir up our hearts, O Lord . . .' says the Vicar. The Collect reminds Caroline that

THE SAGITTARIUS SLOANE

November 23rd, enter the Sagittarius Sloane

Admit it, you *are* a bit naive. Also insanely optimistic. You actually think people *want* to hear the truth about themselves. You blurt it out and then they go and get offended. No wonder you like travelling.

The Sagittarian Sloane sees the world as his/her oyster. More than likely it *has* a pearl in it. It doesn't seem fair, but nice things always do seem to happen to Sloane Sagittarians. You fall in love with the wrong people – but you marry the right one; you can be an irresponsible gambler – but you always win . . . practically.

How can people spend every summer in Norfolk? Check the backgrounds of successful officers and happy Army wives, raid the Sloane hotels, boats, villas in the remotest corners of the earth and chances are you will turn up a strong contingent of bright-eyed, enthusiastic Sagittarians. They never get world-weary.

If you do have to stick to one place, you don't really feel tied to it. You could never be accused of being house-proud. And as for children – the older the better. Babies? Seen one, seen them all. Sloane Sagittarians are horse people, dog people, cat people. Their favourite Christmas character is the pantomime horse. As for the rest of the family, it's lovely to see them – whenever you *do* see them. And friends? They have to be good-natured, clever – and never expect letters.

Your secret: Whether it's food, wine, travelling, lovers – it's a struggle to remember that more is not always better.

it's Stir-Up Sunday (the 25th after Trinity). She whizzes home, girding her coins (20p and 5p bits) to drop in the Christmas pudding mixture – a traditional (alcoholic) family recipe. She adds the bachelor's button, Woolworth wedding ring and spinster's thimble, grabs Henry – or Jack – to stir for luck.

The freezer is ready for the first pheasants of the year. Early in the season, Caroline plucks them, but by the time they are hanging in dozens in the larder, she surreptitiously takes them to the butcher: 'I'm too pushed to do them myself' (20 minutes a bird).

November is the traditional time for killing Jacob lambs. They taste much better if hung ten days. Vanessa had a little lamb and Caroline buys it from her, driving over to have lunch and natter before returning with the carcass. The butcher cuts it up and you spend hours bagging, labelling and shovelling it away in the freezer. (You may buy, bag and freeze a piglet any time during the year. There's no pig-killing season. The piglet will be christened Oink, Snort or Wee, in typical Sloanethink). Sloanes aren't just unsqueamish, they're *religious* about killing. It's 'We kill them because we love them – you don't'. Or, 'We love to kill, we kill to live, we live to love.' Sloanes see killing and eating animals as part of the cycle, but they must do it themselves – they loathe the thought of slaughterhouses and animals suffering.

Snow report

Hail and hearty

The Ski Show at Earl's Court (mid-November). Most Sloanes go twice. Lots of sexy 'Hello! It's John. I met you in Val.' A popular time is Wednesday evening, when the City races are run on the dry ski slope in the middle – Sophie cheers the Lloyd's team captained by ski insurance expert Michael Pettifer.

Sloane tour operators recruit their longest-serving chalet girls to man their stands. A punter's rediscovery of his chalet girl is an emotional moment, with much hugging and reminiscing about 'the time we threw your chocolate mousse into Robin's ski boots'.

After the show, Sloanes disperse in groups to neighbouring restaurants for dinner: the Pontevecchio (nearest, but full of dreadful Northern caravan salesmen from the Caravan and Camping Show, which coincides at Earl's Court), San Quintino and the Hollywood Road Bistro Vino.

Out with the glasses and on with the nouveau Beauj at the Ski Show

From Caroline's Diary

Sent out invitations C'mas party, 6 weeks before and all at once. BOOK PERM.

Found tortoise hidden in a clump of Michaelmas daisies and put her in a hay-box for the winter.

To Eton for Wall Game. V. boring and v. cold – envied the mink coats Jamie is so sniffy about. No score for the 71st year. After the game (H enjoyed it) to see Jamie's large useful wooden bookshelf on display in School Hall. He dying to get rid of us – his Heathfield hope coming over for the reel dance.

Really keen SRs attend avant-ski classes run by Nicole Glynn (Oxford 891004). They are held twice a week in a church hall in central London. More men than women assures a good après-ski scene, since the class goes to the pub afterwards.

November is also the time for the chalet-girl briefings. These are day seminars held in the Hurlingham Club, etc. You are taught basic accountancy and your company's policy on chalet girl vs. guests. There may be an Army-style distribution of Puffa jackets. New-girl friendships started on this day can last a lifetime.

On Henry's mind

• Shooting pheasant and woodcock. (When the leaves are gone, the Sloanes get going.) Charles Clore's old gamekeeper, asked what he thought was the reason for his longevity, said 'Whenever I hear the call "Woodcock" I fall flat on my face.'

• Order game books for Christmas for self, bro-in-law and Mr Tokyokonta: Antony Atha Publishers, Weybread Lodge, nr Diss, Norfolk (037 986 711). (He makes up the pages to suit your shooting, eg if, like the Duke of Marlborough, your estate is crawling with pheasants, he can give you five columns on pheasants.)

Considers ordering 'If it flies it dies' in gold on the cover for bro-in-law, as an American Sloane did, but remember his sense of humour (none).

Forward planning

★ Pantomime, ballet or theatre tickets for Christmas hols. Enrol London youngs in the Unicorn Theatre club, Great Newport Street, WC2 (240 2076)
★ Dentist appointments ditto
★ Photographer ditto, for Christmas presents Granny etc.

DECEMBER

Days 8 hr 1½ min (av), but on the turn
* Royal Smithfield Show, Earl's Court, first week (where the fatstock men meet the fat Stock Exchange men)
* Christmas bazaars and charity balls.
* School carol service
* International Horse Show, Olympia (another must for the teenage horsies)
* Varsity soccer match, Wembley (some public schools including Eton do play what the others call yoik ball – though in *rugger* shorts)
* Varsity rugger match, Twickenham (the City hit by one-day flu. Young Sloanes: hip-flasks and the Cabbage Patch pub opposite the station; wrinklies: hip-flasks and the West Bar)
* UCCA forms filled in for summer A-levels
* Christmas holidays start, around 14th
* Oxbridge entrance results and interviews
* Carol concert, Albert Hall
* Nine-lesson-and-carol service King's College Chapel, Cambridge: watch on the box
* Shortest day (22nd, 1983; 21st, 1984)
* Christmas Day, 25th
* Boxing Day, 26th (better than Christmas. Sporting Sloanes agonise – which? Racing at Kempton Park – George VI Chase; the Queen Mother usually goes. Shooting everywhere; the Queen's family shoots. Hunting everywhere – the merry Boxing Day Meet. Drinks parties everywhere)
* New Year's Eve, 31st (Should auld acquaintance not be drunk, he's no a friend o' mine, we'll kiss each other's husbands noo, for the sake of auld lang syne)

National Hunt racing

Sticks and stones and broken bones
First week in August to first week in June
Sloanes, led by the Queen Mother, far prefer National Hunt racing to the Flat. A Sticks Sloane recently dumped her boyfriend because he got a job as assistant to a flat trainer: 'Those snobs talk about money and racing – never horses.'

November to April is the strong part of the season – the Hennessy Cup to the Whitbread. You can get to know the jumpers. They usually start at four or five and can go on to sixteen. Flat horses flash across one's television screen for two years and then they're gone to stud – or to the zoo for tiger meat. 'They aren't proper horses,' Caroline says, after her first half-hip-flask.

They could move into jumping and *become* proper horses, as Red Rum did. One woman owner was so cross when Lord Oaksey wrote that her Derby entry had a wonderful future over hurdles that she consulted her solicitor. He said you can't libel a horse. So when she saw John Oaksey at Sandown, she trounced him with her handbag.

There is a major hurdle to overcome in the jumping season: it's in the winter. The rich like the flat because they're the Soft. The rich are different from you and me: they don't wear thermal underwear. They are ignorant of the ham-sandwich – whisky – adrenalin cocktail. And they'll never know the love and admiration you feel for the sheer courage and cleverness of horses like Red Rum, Crudwell (he won even after a doping gang had 'stopped' him), Baulking Green, Spartan Missile. (Sloanes adore cleverness in *horses*.)

These are established heroes. But you also like to follow a horse's career. Increasingly, jumpers have both parents in the Stud Book. He (or she) may start as a hunter with your local pack, do two seasons of point-to-points. At, say, seven, you enter him in a hunter chase under National Hunt rules. His professional career begins with a handicap race. He has to be with a trainer, but you can get a private licence to train your own horse(s). He goes on doing well. To qualify him for a big race, he has to win a smaller race worth a certain amount. You enter him at Kelso or Newton Abbot or Taunton or somewhere there won't be too many keen eyes. He wins, but only by half a length. When he starts in

From Caroline's Diary

After finishing the C'mas shopping, discovered the things I got in the Jan sales.

Carol concert at the school. Hanky completely sopped by 'mild, obedient, good as He'.

the big race it should be at long odds, so you and your friends can, you hope, make a killing.

Newbury is a deeply Sloane jumping course (the November meeting). March is the best Sloane month, with the Grand Military and Imperial Cup at Sandown (Army and Army groupies), followed by Cheltenham (Irish priests betting in rolls of £50 notes), followed by the Grand National (giant jumps, slow horses. 'The Elephant Marathon').

From Caroline's Diary

HOLS START. Cooking takes mind off what else is in the Christmas post as we wait for Jamie's Oxbridge results. He says if you hear before C'mas you're in, if not, not.

End-of-term reports. Edward 'not academic tho one of the nicest boys in the school'. Alas for his future. Emma more promising.

Henry at yet another Lloyd's party. Told him it's ridiculous the way they drink like schoolboys, tell schoolboy jokes and then fall on secretaries half their age (ie 8).

From Caroline's Diary

Visited Anthony at Harrods. The other side of the counter sounds horrendous. The regular staff bag the good customers and elderly homosexuals come round looking for a boy for their stocking.

All Sophie's and J's friends seem to be there. Harry P specialises in sinking to his knees under the counter pretending he is going downstairs to the stockroom, then slowly rising to tell the customer it's out of stock!

Snow report

Nine inches, and lying

Chalet girls go out to the Alps a week or two before the punters to clean up the chalets and secure cheap rates at the night-clubs. ('Je m'appelle Sophie et je travail pour Bladon Lines d'Angleterre. Est-ce que c'est possible d'avoir les boissons libres si je promets de vous apporter tous mes clients?' Begging in a foreign language sounds quite acceptable to Sophie's ear.

Je m'appelle Sarah Lumley, fille de chalet

Yum Yum, Piggy's Bum

HOORAY PUDDING SAUCE

It has to be schoolboy puddings at this time of the year, to keep out the cold. (Caroline never dares touch them herself but the Hoorays adore them. She has to make the effort, or Henry will be driven into the arms of his club.) This sauce goes extremely well on Bread and Butter Pudding, left-over Christmas Pudding, Treacle Sponge and what used to be called Spotted Dick (whatever can we call it now?). Henry's once-a-week tart is Treacle.

For 4

8 tbsp unsalted butter ● 8 tbsp icing sugar ● 1 egg ● whisky to taste

In a double boiler stir the butter and sugar together until the sugar has dissolved and the mixture is very hot. Beat the egg, then whisk it into the hot mixture, away from the heat. Beat until it has cooled to room temperature, then add whisky. Cut the pudding into helpings. Spoon the sauce over each one and heat it a moment or two under the grill.

BREAD AND BUTTER PUDDING

For 4

Knob unsalted butter ● 6 slices of bread and butter (any kind of bread, crusts off) ● 1 handful mixed dried fruit ● 2 eggs (large) ● 1 tbsp sugar mixed with ½ tsp mixed spice or cinnamon ● 1 pint milk

Butter a pie dish, generously. Fill it with layers of bread and butter interspersed with the dried fruit. (The Prince of Wales's version is said to include slices of banana and gobbets of black treacle at this point.) Beat the eggs with the sugar and spice. Add the milk (Prince Charles adds brandy to taste as well). Pour it over the pudding and leave it to soak in for about half an hour, or longer. Cover the top loosely with foil or paper and bake it in a low oven (275°F, gas 1) for an hour and a half in all, taking the paper off for the last half hour so that the top browns. Serve with cream and more sugar, or with Hooray sauce.

GLÜHWEIN

No Sloane Christmas would be complete without glühwein, the modern wassail. Sloanes discovered it skiing. Never tastes the same of course. Fear, the essential ingredient, is missing.

For a party

Tip into a large saucepan:

As many bottles of red plonk as needed (No Emma, *not* Daddy's claret) ● A goodly splash of rum ● A handful of cloves and cinnamon sticks (foodie Sloanes add cardoman) ● Brown sugar to taste ● Slices of lemon and orange.

Keep on low heat until all flavours are diffused. Serve in large wine glasses (no burnt fingers). The second most depressing thing about Christmas is relentless glühwein drinking. The first is tepid glühwein. KEEP IT HOT.

From mid-December until mid-April, Geneva Airport on a Saturday is a Sloane social centre. About ten Sloane charter flights fly in and out of Geneva every week and exponential encounters take place on the moving walkways. A pale incoming Sloane finds himself approaching a bronzed homebound Sloane he once met at a dinner party. He shouts 'Where did you go?' 'What's the snow like?' 'What are the chalet girls like?' *'Amazing* – there's one called Sophie . . .' (– but by this time Henry Bronzé is out of Henry Pale's earshot).

The rendezvous point is the bar downstairs in the Arrivals Hall, where glasses of Fendant are bought with French francs at a deeply disadvan-tageous exchange rate. Unfortunately, there is no departures board down here, and some punters enjoying their last few minutes with their chalet girl find they have missed their charter flight.

Sloanes do not understand charter flights. Skiing is one of the very few occasions they use them, and they in-furiate airlines like British Caledonian, British Midland and Dan-Air by not believing that if they miss their charter flight they have to *buy* another ticket, with no refund on the charter ticket.

December is the month for really keen skiers, who can't wait to get out on to the first snow. It also draws raunchy Henrys who can't wait to get out on to the chalet girls while they are fresh and naïve.

it in January – they come back like lightning). The winter jasmine is coming out, and the Old Blush China is still flowering. It's the original 'last rose of summer'.

Thank goodness the holly has done you proud with berries. It isn't the same having to buy it. You line the tops of the picture frames and crown the pud (but a front-door wreath is very non-U).

From now until the end of February is a bad time for the poor birds. You hang bacon rind, coconut halves, strings of nuts etc, on a low branch if you haven't a bird table. A bag of mixed seeds suits grain-eating birds, including doves (Henry says doves are 'bloody pigeons', and of course he's right).

But Sloanes have a special, natural sympathy for those fellow creatures who prefer to catch their food live. The wild birds around Sloanes who breed meal-worms become very friendly. (It is also a good way to ensure that one's only visitors are other Sloanes.)

Larder and freezer

Mince pies are only the tip of the freezerberg. You spend days cooking and filling it with lasagne etc, so you can spend the rest of the month serving and washing up all day while the children are at home eating all day.

Sloane Christmas presents

New jokes in old paper

Caroline buys 90 per cent of the family presents. Henry buys 5 per cent. The children make 2½ per cent and buy 2½ per cent (they're generous – anticipating an overdraft by a few years). Sloanes don't say gifts, always presents (or pressies). Other people have polluted the word gifts.

Caroline acts as information exchange. Sloanes expect to stock up on what they need at Christmas, it's one of

Geneva airport: Supertravel reps await the avalanche of punters

There is very little naïvety left in any chalet by the end of the season.

Other December people are families (Sloane parents know taking them skiing will bring the horrors back to heel), and bachelor City types, who 'find it easier to take leave over the public holiday' (have been clever enough to escape the parental Christmas). When the going gets tough, the tough go skiing.

The garden and larder

Little doing in the garden

Wickedly cold. Caroline sends off for next year's seed catalogues (you can do

From Caroline's Diary

Sigh of relief. Jamie's in! He and H thrilled. But the thought of him off to Australia for 9 months is not pleasant. It's not really a Gap in their lives, it's leaping into the unknown and all the dangers.

My green silk has been revisiting ten years of ballrooms and ladies' rooms. Sophie sick all day after Feathers.

Wish people would print their names on their C cards, particularly the ones saying Arriving on 3rd.

December

the economies. 'I want it to be a surprise' is not Sloane.

Caro did her shopping a month ago, spending two days in London on that and the perm (Robert Fielding in Sloane Street, the Cadogan Club, or if she's decided to Do Something About Herself, perhaps Leonard or Xavier).

Granny and godparents give you white envelopes in which is a cheque, a book token or a record token. The white envelopes are depended on, and so is the champagne/claret from grandfather/Uncle Howard. If it didn't arrive you'd be in the shoup (or the cranberry saush, sinch it'sh Chrismash).

Sloane presents outside the information range are fairly useless though rarely cheap (never be seen to be mean – fall back on a big Badedas). They are either swallowable, smellable or amusing. Presents for town-dwellers have country-sports motifs, presents for country-dwellers naked bodies or politicians.

Henry also receives tweedy gumboot socks, Caroline photograph frames. The children give them jokes (rude food, huge lighters, machines that go squark in fridges and loos). Sloane children of two to 42 wake up on Christmas Day to bulging stockings.

Sloanes agonise to all their chums about how much to give the milkman, postman, dustbinmen, keeper (not spoiling the market is essential). Henry gives the keeper £20 and a bottle of port. He would rather have had whisky and

THE CAPRICORN SLOANE

December 22nd, enter the Capricorn Sloane

Cool, collected, cautious Capricorn … Non-Sloanes might even call you cold. But you just find it hard to express your feelings. You prefer to stay quietly in the background, observing.

Your head rules your heart. You don't really think there is anything wrong with an arranged marriage. The idea of a wild infatuation is pathetic: what matters is compatibility of background, tradition, income. Your sensitivity takes the form of knowing what is right for the occasion. Others may see this as snobbery or social climbing. You see it as realism.

You're an industrious worker, emulating your elders and betters. Even as a child you were always happier with older people. You like their seriousness, their achievements, their *success*. Male or female, you're often seen as paternalistic, Victorian. But that is the only way to make sure that people – and children are people – reach their true potential. And any child of yours has potential.

Capricorn Sloanes are not *mad* about food – cooking it or eating out. It doesn't do to get too carried away with these sensual appetites. And drink – well, it's fun, but you more than pay for it with that ghastly getting-up-all-night business. The thing that gives you most sensual enjoyment is music; you can get quite soppy at the love scene in *La Bohème*.

Your secret: To be perfectly honest, the only time you're *really* relaxed is when you're alone with Labby.

makes Henry walking gun and sends him through the boggy bits.

Sloane presents still have the price on them. They are appallingly wrapped up. Some of the paper and ribbon has creases from the last present it wrapped. To do up all your presents in the same paper and tie with ornate loops of shiny ribbon is Mayfair Merc, Artistic or noovo.

Emma to Edward

God I HATE Christmas!

Today we had to go to those grotty carols at the Albert Hall. Had a row with Mummie about wearing Grandpa's old trilby. She said it was sacrilegious, stupid old bag. Wore it anyway. Jamie didn't arrive until after O Come All Ye Faithful (lots of filthy looks from the wrinklies). Brought that boring girlfriend of his. Don't know why he bothers, she's so ugly. The Bach choir sang endless things in French and Latin. Can't think why they don't sing them in English. You have to have about five million O levels just to understand carols. Guess who I saw?? Freddie Munro!! In a suit!!!! Introduced me to his dad who is quite dishy, for an old man.

After the interval had to endure the little kids singing Away in a Manger on stage (the Grown Ups think it's sweet of course). David Willcocks made the same joke about who could sing louder, the boys or the girls. He must get really bored, he should know

by now the girls always do. Some creep from North London won the carol competition, he looked a real swot. Actually the carol was OK. For a carol.

At long last we sang Hark the Herald Angels Sing/Beecham Pills Are Just the Thing/Peace on Earth and Motion Mild/Two for an Adult, one for a Child (more filthy looks). Dad sang really flat and Mummie tried to sing the descant (god, parents are an embarrassment).

Went to the Russells' tea afterwards. Everyone asked what I was doing. Pretty dumb question – what else can you do at twelve apart from school? Amanda was there in the most revolting green velvet skirt, plus that repellent brother of hers with slimy hands. Anyway Mr Munro said he loved my hat which was yaa boo sucks to the Dragon. Thank God for once he didn't say I looked like her. Fiona says older men are much more exciting. But I'm not too sure about the bald patches.

Ate too much cake. So much for the diet.

God I LOVE glühwein!

From Caroline's Diary

To Scotland 27th, thank goodness. Did the usual flop into parental mattress.

Dec 31. Hogmanay. Pa doesn't change – asked Ed for tenth time where he could see a man with as many noses as there are days in the year . . . stayed up all night.

On Henry's mind

See out the old
- Firm's financial year ends (the Government's financial year ending in April is a hangover from farming. Most businesses wind up in either December or March).
- The office parties. In the City you don't just go to your own firm's annual debauch, but all the others as well – so business dicey for the last two weeks of the month.
- The breathalyser.
- Buying Christmas presents (afternoon of 23rd or 24th).
- After Christmas, review next year's banker's orders in time to cut out unwanted 1 Jan payments. Leave the £15 a month to New & Lingwood – paying for shirts on the slow drip.

Forward planning

★ After Christmas, book table Aintree for the National (p 40)

Micalago and Campden Park. Sloanes immediately feel at home in the Scone house, which follows the same Georgian-is-best principle as the Sloane counterpart, with a few differences – fewer flowery chintzes (too precious for the Aussie bush), lots of *modern* art. Visually, Scones tend to be more sophisticated than Sloanes. Modern Australian painters like Sidney Nolan are OK in a way that would be totally wrong in the Old Rectory in Wiltshire.

However, Jamie is not there for the art, especially in the summer (January). In between jackerooing (he says he's on wombat duty) he goes to the Test Match and to Palm Beach, the smart seaside place north of Sydney which used to be Scones' alone. He gets to Adelaide in March (festival, stately homes) and back to Sydney for Easter (the Royal Easter Show – agrifun – and polo). The great Scone Ranger thing is Picnic Races. Aussie landowners match their best horses against each other. Strictly amateur, competitors travel hundreds of miles for the races and the hooleys that follow. There's always a ball on the night of the Picnics , followed by another – the 'Recovery' – the following night.

Skiing and the social season start in June (winter). Spring arrives in September. Jamie inveigles himself out to the coast: the FFNQ ('Fuckin' Far North Queensland). He wishes he could go to the Melbourne Cup in November, but he has to return to England. He has been remembering to (tele)phone Sloane.

Jamie arrives back in England in September wearing a bush hat. He annoys Henry and Caroline by saying 'Gooday' instead of 'Good morning,' at breakfast, but up at Oxford he reverts to good old OE Hooray Henry-in-the-making.

If you want to know what life will be like for him, turn this book the right way up and go back to the beginning.

THE NEXT YEAR

The Scone Ranger

The Sloane Down Under

Sloanes love to spend time Down Under. New Zealand is the Sloane place but they usually go to Australia (more money). Wrinkles go for just a few weeks (and add to their wrinkles), but Jamie flies off after Christmas on a make-a-man-of-you six-to-nine-month tour between school and Oxford. Prince Charles did it; Prince Edward did it. Even healthy little Sloanes do it. Let's do it, let's go to Scone (a horsy, Sloany farming town in New South Wales).

Before he goes, Jamie canvasses all his muckers and plagues Henry, Caroline and the relations for contacts. These have to be good for a) a free bed for the night (or for six months) or b) getting him a job as a jackeroo (station hand). Jamie collates reams of addresses into geographic order – so it's off to Sydney by Qantas (Quaint Arse).

The Sloane suburbs of Sydney are Double Bay ('Double pay' – it's the Beverly Hills of Australia) and Paddington (the largest area of unspoilt Victorian terrace houses in the world, with a restaurant called The Sloane Ranger). Paddington is the Fulham of Australia. Sloanespeak is the main language; Strine sounds as incongruous as it does in the Royal Enclosure at Ascot.

Jamie has a copy of the List – an unofficial Aussie Social Register of all the Scone Rangers he should meet. However, these top Australians have been hit too often not to be wary of the prowling, bumming Sloane. The first contact with Scones should be presold by at least one letter from a reliable mutual friend in England. Otherwise the answer could be: 'We're terribly sorry, we'll be in Port Douglas that weekend.'

Scone on the range

Anyone who saw *My Brilliant Career* also saw in some detail the inside of two of Australia's most famous Scone houses –

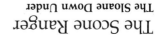

ACKNOWLEDGEMENTS

The authors and the publishers are grateful to the following for permission to reproduce their photographs: Nigel Allsop 31, 34, 37, 48, 51, 67, 84, 88, 107, 108, 120; Associated Newspapers 119; Sue Carpenter 10, 11, 15, 35, 61, 75, 77, 90; Tim Carpenter 33; William Clark 69; Nicholas Coleridge 121; Alan Davidson/Alpha 45; Dick Evans 56, 57, 63, 67, 69; Jenny Fabian 38; Tim Graham 12, 20, 70; Kit Houghton 28; Anwar Hussein 54, 86; Alex James 18, 23, 25, 88, 99, 103, 104/105; Photo Reportage 95; Bryan Poole 105; Alistair Scott 123; Scottish Tourist Board 96, 97, 99; James Shand 91; Roger Sharpe 106; Sporting Pictures 27; Chris Stonehill 19; Homer Sykes 17, 59; Simon Taylor 72; Times Newspapers 44/45, 62, 81; Araminta ffaulls-Tooth 125; Jill Tyler 85; Sophy Webster 36; Michael Yardley 40, 41, 43, 65, 101, 113; Tara Yardley 29.

The front cover photographs, left to right: Tim Graham, Stanley Hurwitz, Alex James; frame by Lucy Askew; ragged background by Jackie Horsford; photographic reproduction by Photodesign.